Race and the American Story

Race and the American Story

STEPHANIE SHONEKAN

AND

ADAM SEAGRAVE

OXFORD
UNIVERSITY PRESS

OXFORD
UNIVERSITY PRESS

Oxford University Press is a department of the University of Oxford. It furthers
the University's objective of excellence in research, scholarship, and education
by publishing worldwide. Oxford is a registered trade mark of Oxford University
Press in the UK and certain other countries.

Published in the United States of America by Oxford University Press
198 Madison Avenue, New York, NY 10016, United States of America.

Library of Congress Cataloging-in-Publication Data
Names: Shonekan, Stephanie, author. | Seagrave, Adam, author.
Title: Race and the American story / Stephanie Shonekan and Adam Seagrave.
Description: New York, NY : Oxford University Press, [2024] |
Includes bibliographical references and index. |
Contents: Black, White, Human—Two
Experiences, One Nation—Knowledge and Ignorance—The Road to
the Future—Freedom and Hope, Liberation and Love.
Identifiers: LCCN 2023046753 | ISBN 9780197767696 (pb) | ISBN 9780197767689 (hb) |
ISBN 9780197767719 (epub) | ISBN 9780197767726 (ebook)
Subjects: LCSH: African Americans—History. | Racism—United States—History. |
United States—Race relations—History. | African American intellectuals—History. |
African American musicians—History. | Shonekan, Stephanie.
Classification: LCC E185 .S49 2024 | DDC 305.800973—dc23/eng/20231103
LC record available at https://lccn.loc.gov/2023046753

DOI: 10.1093/oso/9780197767689.001.0001

Paperback printed by Marquis Book Printing, Canada
Hardback printed by Bridgeport National Bindery, Inc., United States of America

For Summer
—Adam

For Faramola, Ojurere, and Mojuba
—Stephanie

CONTENTS

ACKNOWLEDGMENTS

We thank the many colleagues at Mizzou and elsewhere who contributed to the Race and the American Story project in its early days and have supported it over the years, including April Langley, Justin Dyer, Rudy Hernandez, Scott Brooks, Charles Hughes, Aram Goudsouzian, and Nicholas Buccola. We are especially grateful to the hundreds of students at Mizzou, University of Massachusetts at Amherst, Arizona State University, and other institutions who have given their time, talent, and energy to understanding race in America and their fellow students through participation in the Race and the American Story course and activities. The example of these students has been a source of constant inspiration and motivation. We are grateful for Susan Kells, who has worked hard on making our Race and the American Story symposium successful.

We also thank our editor, David McBride, for working so skillfully and diligently with us throughout the review process. The anonymous reviewers provided excellent feedback for which we are very grateful.

Adam thanks Peter Onuf, whose generous insight and advice were invaluable in guiding the development of this book. Nicholas Buccola and Robert Saldin were very helpful in finding the right publisher. Adam especially thanks his wife, Rosie, for her advice and encouragement as one of the book's very early readers, as well as for her essential support throughout the writing process.

Stephanie is thankful for her sister-scholar friends—Sheri Harrison, Keona Ervin, and Cristina Mislan—who have encouraged her to keep writing, in the midst of her administrative role. She is also grateful for the love and support of her husband, Tomiwa, for his unwavering support and advice to continue growing and dreaming.

Adam and Stephanie are grateful for each other. It goes without saying that this kind of project requires a special partnership to listen to and learn from each other, and to ultimately grow as scholars and human beings. We are thankful for the patience, candor, and sincerity that we have cultivated over the years that results in this fruitful friendship and partnership on all the dimensions of the Race and the American Story project.

Introduction

"Have we the will as a nation to exorcise the one [racism] and evoke the other [freedom]? In order for us, Black and white, to disenthrall ourselves from the harshest slave-master, racism, we must disinter our buried history."[1] In 2015, the University of Missouri experienced a collective awakening when Black students raised the issue of racism on campus, in the city of Columbia, and in the state of Missouri. Across the United States, Trayvon Martin, Tamir Rice, Sandra Bland, Eric Garner, and so many other African Americans had all been killed within a couple of years of each other.[2] In Ferguson, Missouri, an unarmed Michael Brown was shot by the police, his body left in the street for hours. On campus, students were called the N word regularly, and they had to avoid walking through Greek town. A decade earlier, cotton balls had been strewn on the lawn in front of the Gaines-Oldham Black Culture Center. Black students at Mizzou, burdened with the unrelenting trauma that had piled up from one generation to another, carefully and thoughtfully organized a series of marches and raised loud, urgent, reverberating questions about what the faculty, staff, administration, and board of curators were doing to push back against the tide of racism.[3] They were joined by student allies and a collective of faculty and staff who stood by in support. After a hunger strike, a boycott by football players, and a confused administration, the president and chancellor stepped down and there were new measures and jobs created to improve inclusion, diversity, and equity on the campus.

Race and the American Story. Stephanie Shonekan and Adam Seagrave, Oxford University Press.
© Oxford University Press 2024. DOI: 10.1093/oso/9780197767689.003.0001

One of the outcomes of the movement was the need for a training program for all students. It was clear to many of us that this program could not be an online training as was done for the Title IX and alcohol awareness programs. We insisted on an in-person program where we could really engage students face-to-face. Stephanie worked with a few colleagues to design a two-hour orientation program for all incoming students. This program, called Citizenship@Mizzou, used live music curated and performed by a group of students, and faculty sharing brief narratives about their understandings of the university values of respect, responsibility, discovery, and excellence. Stephanie's students formed a band, Talking Drum, and worked with her to select the popular music that could help drive the conversations around these values. Talking Drum played songs like Bob Dylan's "Blowin' in the Wind" to help us talk about the value of respect. Talking Drum played it in a folksy/country acoustic style like Bob Dylan's version of 1963, and then after the first verse, the rest of the band joined the guitar and voice to play the rest of the song as Stevie Wonder covered it in 1966. We asked our new students to consider what the questions were—about humanity, equality, war, and the environment—that were still "blowin' in the wind," and whether the questions were different when they were asked by one or the other artist, in one or the other style.

Other songs Talking Drum played for Citizenship@Mizzou were John Lennon's "Imagine" (1971) and Marvin Gaye's "What's Going On" (1970) to discuss the value of discovery; Michael Jackson's "Man in the Mirror" (1988) to get to the heart of responsibility; and Queen Latifah's "I Know Where I've Been," from the musical *Hairspray* (2007), to exemplify the value of excellence. All in all, this program was successful. We recognized that our students come from different parts of the state and the country as well as the world. They were from rural areas, urban spaces, college towns, and suburbs. They arrived on campus with different worldviews and beliefs. How could we expect them to bond seamlessly without reminding them of the incredible value and great potential of our distinct identities contributing to the building of a single university community, into a Mizzou we could all share?

Evaluations of the Citizenship@Mizzou program were mostly positive. Of course, there was that group of students who came in scowling, sat with their arms crossed, and slowly dropped the scowl and the arms as the music hit their ears. Most of them sat up and joined the discussion about the music and the values. There was also a handful of students who seemed to remain unmoved and unwilling to engage. But the majority seemed to enjoy it. One reaction we got a lot from students was that this two-hour program was just scratching the surface and that there was so much more to talk about. For instance, as we talk about the 1960s and 1970s reflected in "Blowin in the Wind," there is so much about American history and culture that we don't have time to get to. There is no time to discuss the complexities of the Vietnam War or the civil rights and Black Power movements. This time crunch was something we could not get away from. Citizenship@Mizzou was better than an online course but not as good as a full semester course.

When Adam approached Stephanie to collaborate on a new course, both agreed that there was an opportunity to extend the potential of Citizenship@Mizzou. We could provide students with an opportunity to delve more deeply into the histories that were influenced by and reflected in the music that inspired the original Citizenship@Mizzou program. We could, moreover, help them to do this together, in conversations with one another that allowed them to walk together from ignorance to awareness, from confusion to comprehension, from fear to confidence, as they encountered stories from American history that illuminated and validated their own. This first conversation about our potential collaboration was the starting point for a highly successful course and project. It was also a kind of endpoint of each of our personal journeys of discovery—including, importantly, self-discovery—that had led each of us to think and care about issues of race in America. Geographically, it was also a kind of midpoint between the beginning of Stephanie's story in Nigeria, and the beginning of Adam's story in California. This book describes our individual journeys to that moment, conceived in each of these ways. Each of us came to that moment having thought and taught about race. We were ready to imagine what a world would look like where we were aware of and knowledgeable about our history, moved by those stories, and, armed with new revelations and convictions, prepared to shape a new path to racial and social justice.

Race and the American Story, as we decided to call the class, would help our students and faculty across the campus to understand the roots of our difficult conversations about race. It would provide them with the historical and conceptual knowledge necessary to formulate accurate opinions about past and current problems. Most importantly, it would engage students who often stuck to themselves and studied different disciplines—and who had different ethnic or racial backgrounds—in the same reading material, the same questions, and, most crucially, even in the same classroom discussions with each other. It would extend and magnify the impact of Citizenship@Mizzou across an entire semester, building on it in ways we hoped would bring healing to a campus sorely in need of it.

The Race and the American Story class is not your average college course on issues of racial and social justice. In fact, it was and remains in many ways the first and only course of its kind in the country. Its uniqueness stems from its process of development, from its focus on particular historical and conceptual content, and from its distinctive goals. Drawing an essential musical thread from Citizenship@Mizzou, the course challenges our students to also think about how musicians have framed the evolving concept of race in the American story.

Most college courses are the product of a single professor's approach and expertise. Some college courses involve collaborations between two or more faculty members who share overlapping interests and complementary scholarly backgrounds. Race and the American Story grew out of a campus crisis and from roots situated on opposite sides of a vast social and academic divide. Stephanie was chair of the Black Studies Department, and Adam was a faculty member in the Department of Political Science and affiliated with the Kinder Institute on Constitutional Democracy. The faculty and students in Stephanie's department studied the histories and experiences of people of Africa and the African diaspora. The faculty and students in Adam's department studied American political history and development, with a particular emphasis on the American Founding. The vast majority of the faculty and students in Stephanie's department were people of African ancestry themselves. The vast majority of faculty and students in Adam's department were people of European ancestry. In different parts of campus we had Black folks studying the history and culture of Black folks, and white folks studying the history and culture of white folks. For one of these groups, America's birth date was 1619; for the other, it was 1776. No single college course, or other educational endeavor of which we are aware, has been the product of a collaboration between faculty leaders representing two campus groups so diametrically opposed along deeply sensitive and controversial fault lines.[4] Our class would build bridges between parts of campus, and parts of American society, that seemed oceans apart.

The first of these bridges to be constructed was between the faculty members in Stephanie's and Adam's departments. We knew that our collaboration would have the greatest impact if it included an organizational partnership between our respective units; enjoying the input and endorsement of both unit leaders, and including the contributions of additional faculty members within each unit. We convened a group of six faculty members—three from the Department of Black Studies (including Stephanie), and three from the Kinder Institute on Constitutional Democracy (including Adam)—and together we codesigned a single core syllabus that constituted about 75 percent of an average college course. The remaining 25 percent would be filled out according to individual faculty preference. This new course was cross-listed with Political Science, History, and Black Studies.

The fact that a course on issues of race in American history successfully emerged out of a collaboration between white and Black faculty members, from different departments, at the University of Missouri—a major epicenter of racial tension, particularly at that time—was a minor miracle. Looking back on this feat five years later, it appears even more improbable than it did at the time. This unlikely process of development made a distinctive mark on the shape of the course itself. The faculty members from Black Studies wanted readings from the perspective of enslaved African Americans at the time of the American Founding; faculty members from the Kinder Institute wanted readings by white

American Founders. Faculty from Black Studies wanted readings on the failures of Reconstruction; faculty from the Kinder Institute wanted readings on the successful outcome of the Civil War. Faculty from Black Studies wanted readings from W. E. B. Du Bois, Ida Wells, and Malcolm X; faculty from the Kinder Institute wanted readings from Frederick Douglass, Booker T. Washington, and Martin Luther King Jr. What we all discovered during this process was that there was, in fact, a place for all of these perspectives in the course we were building. Each of the faculty members involved in this process emerged from it with a more accurate and complete understanding of race in American history than we had when the process began. The same, we believe, is true of our students who take the course.

Another distinctive feature of the Race and the American Story course—and it has become a point of even greater distinctiveness in the time since its creation—is its focus on American historical primary sources.[5] Nearly every college and university has courses on African American history, African American politics, anti-Black racism, and related topics. Nearly every college and university also has nonacademic administrative trainings or minicourses that focus on racism, prejudice, or implicit bias. All such courses and trainings we have encountered in our experience, however, rely heavily, if not exclusively, on secondary texts and authors from the late twentieth and early twenty-first centuries.[6] All of the readings in the Race and the American Story core syllabus are primary sources, and all but a few are dated prior to the 1970s. This is not because we believe that nothing of value has been written on the topic of race in the past fifty years; it is because we believe historical perspective to be fundamental for understanding the present, and that important insights from the past can help lead us to a better future. We also believe that our students can draw their own conclusions about what the primary source documents say about each moment in American history. In this matter of race and racism, it is critical that we all find our way to our individual epiphanies. Unlike other subjects in our classrooms, racism (and other -isms) have deep consequences to real life. Theories and analysis are the bread and butter of the academy, but when a subject has such deeply rooted ramifications, it is worth offering the space for students to think their way to their own groundbreaking, paradigm-shifting awareness.

A further distinctive element of our course's focus on historical primary sources is its prominent inclusion of music. Stephanie is an ethnomusicologist; Adam came from a musical family background, with two piano teachers for parents. We share a deep appreciation for the ways in which music can often provide the clearest and most beautiful window into the societies out of which it emerges, and into our common humanity as well. A music playlist assignment is a mainstay and highlight of the course in its many iterations, and also of our annual symposium gatherings. Including musical texts in our exploration of historical primary sources allows us to explore issues of race in American society even more deeply and engagingly, providing new reflections and outlets for the thoughts and feelings of our students. Music animates history, and the textual primary sources we encounter, making them more alive for us and our students today.

There are, of course, numerous college courses and other educational programs that encourage understanding and dialogue across differences, including racial ones. Such programs of study have similarities with the Race and the American Story course. Our course, though, differs from the vast majority of such programs in its exclusive focus on Black/white racial issues.[7] We have been questioned, pushed, and even challenged on this focus at various times over the years, and we have held to it firmly. As in the case of our historical focus, this focus is not intended to be exclusionary. It is not because we think other differences and the causes associated with them are unimportant. It is because we are convinced of the crucial importance of achieving a deep, focused understanding of Black/white racial issues; and we know that any dilution of this focus risks sowing confusion and diverting us from our primary mission. We are excited to see the good work that has been done on other racial experiences—Latinx,[8] Asian,[9] Indigenous,[10] bi- and multiracial—and on other marginalized identities. As a whole body of intellectual inquiry, we are all pushing our society forward, asking ourselves what it will take for all of us to be treated with respect and dignity. For us—Adam and Stephanie—experiencing the movement at Mizzou, and reflecting on our own identities, we made a decision to stay focused on the enduring Black/white dichotomy in the United States, knowing that revelations made at this locus could also generate space to discuss other identities in the United States and beyond.

The Race and the American Story course also possesses a distinctive twofold goal: to bring about communities of mutual understanding between Black and white Americans by talking together about our shared history. This ambitious goal is what drove our course to become a broader project extending far beyond the college classroom. Our course is about a particular cultural history—American, including African American, history—but it is also about the students who encounter this history together. We aim both to impart historical knowledge and to cultivate new capacities for understanding, caring, and friendship across racial lines. We do this through the conversational method we consistently employ in all Race and the American Story classrooms, and also through the annual symposium to which we invite all students and faculty involved in the course. From the beginning, we conceived the course as the basis for a community of students and faculty that would extend outside the classroom and outlive the space of a single semester. It is both a college course and a community of friends.

This book is an organic reflection of our experiences in conceiving and creating the Race and the American Story course, and it mirrors the course in various ways. Because of this, it speaks in a particular way to college and university communities—to administrators, professors, staff members, and students. Stephanie and Adam have both spent most of their adult lives in various parts of these communities at many different institutions: as undergraduates, graduate students, faculty members, and administrators. The intersections of our personal stories with our experiences as college professors and our expertise as scholars will resonate in a particular way with people who live and work in the world of higher education.

College students are, almost by definition, at a formative time in their lives. Institutions of higher education exist to guide and structure this formative process. Because of this mission, colleges and universities often occupy a vanguard position in forming and reforming society more broadly.

This has been true especially on issues of race and diversity over the past half century with the emerging influence of Black Studies departments, the discipline of ethnic studies, and related areas. In coming out of and speaking to college and university communities, therefore, this is also a book for people outside of these communities who are at a formative moment in their outlook on racial issues.

It has recently seemed as if many Americans of all ages have been forcibly returned to such a moment. The galvanizing event of George Floyd's public murder (along with numerous other visible and similarly jarring events) charged the COVID-era upheaval with a racial awareness that has continued to run through American society like a current, simultaneously shocking, electrifying, and polarizing in ways that have made the tensions and questions of 2015 even more urgently and widely felt. The combination of curiosity about the past, discontent with the present, and hope for the future that often characterizes college students has become far more generalized than usual in recent years. This is both unsettling and comforting; it may not be pleasant to find oneself bereft of clear answers, but an educator recognizes in this situation the essential precondition for genuine learning and real discovery. We hope that our book provides the educative response for which our circumstances so loudly call.

And for those whose hearts have been hardened on racial issues in one way or another, this book is designed to bring about a new formative moment. Its approach is unlikely to resemble anything the reader has encountered before. Try as the reader might, our stories and commentary cannot be shoehorned into one or the other side of recent or historical debates. There are many intersections with previous work on racial issues, to be sure; but the road we travel is our own. These pages contain honest descriptions and personal reflections of the reality of inhuman racism in the United States and around the world. There is no avoidance of harsh realities here; no "yes, but" treatments of racist injustice. This honesty is paired with a kind of optimism; not the sanguine optimism of naivete, but a sober optimism inspired by real human potential for good and a deep-rooted hope that this potential will be increasingly realized in practice. This is a difficult road to map in our contemporary conversations about race, and some readers may initially even find it disorienting or confusing. A new road, though, opens new possibilities for relating to the world in which we find ourselves. It will be up to the reader to decide whether our road is preferable to other, better-traveled ones on offer today.

This book is therefore neither a practitioner's manual nor a directed contribution to a particular academic literature. In the first three chapters, we relate our personal stories to the educational, cultural, and political dynamics that have shaped American life over the past few decades. Chapter 1 recounts Stephanie's and Adam's personal discoveries of what it means to be "Black" or "white," connecting these discoveries to the historical development and implications of these concepts both in the United States and globally. Chapter 2 contains our intersecting perspectives and analyses of racism in the United States, derived both from our experiences as well as from our scholarly expertise in American history and culture. In Chapter 3 we reflect particularly on the role of education in the struggle against racism, on both the personal and social levels. In each of these chapters the narrative periodically alternates between Stephanie's and Adam's perspectives, highlighting the way in which the interaction of diverse experiences and points of view contributes to a fuller understanding of our country, our world, and our humanity.

The final two chapters launch deeper into social and political theory, reflecting on the broader significance of the explorations of human, American, racialized, and personal identity pursued in the first chapters to understanding American history and culture. Chapter 4 takes a close look at recent issues and trends in American society in light of the historical context out of which they have emerged, and argues that a road to a better future can be built with some of the materials we have gathered in this book. Chapter 5 zooms out from recent American society to explore original and striking connections between American historical ideals and the artistic creations of the African diaspora, arguing that these two perhaps unlikely partners join to create a beautiful basis for hope in our common world. Taken all together from beginning to end, we offer a journey from unique personal experience to broad social analysis and back again, in the hope that the reader who follows us on this journey will be inspired to see themselves and their society more clearly and more completely than they did before.

Pursuing these ambitious goals in our own unique way, and in the face of many obstacles, hasn't been easy. We both knew we couldn't just snap our fingers and erase the effects of years, decades, and centuries of injustice, oppression, conflict, disagreement, alienation, and so much else with good intentions and a course packet of readings. Despite the support and assistance of good friends and colleagues at Mizzou from the very beginning, we have both felt at times as if we're pushing a boulder up a steep hill only to see it roll down, time and again. We have both felt at times as if maybe the bridge was actually a mirage, and that really the only ground we can stand on, at the end of day, is the one we started from. And yet we have persevered through these uncertainties, and through career developments that have taken each of us to new places and positions, to continue to build on the foundation we have laid.

More than half a decade later, the Race and the American Story course has been taught by dozens of faculty members to hundreds of students. It is a mainstay on the Mizzou campus, and has expanded to many other universities across the United States and Europe. The trail we blazed after the killing of Mike Brown remains a uniquely promising one after the killing of George Floyd and the renewed racial reckoning that has followed. Our approach is one of honesty but not despair, of realism but not cynicism; it is the approach of understanding, love, and—especially—hope.

Black, White, Human

BECOMING BLACK

I didn't know I was Black until I came to the United States. The journey
to my personal understanding of Blackness has been long and rife with
pain and passion, excitement and exasperation. The fact that the facets
of my identity seem to stretch across the diaspora—Equatorial Guinea,
Nigeria, Trinidad and Tobago, and the United States—means that this
journey has not been straightforward. It has been treacherous, with many
frustrating moments when I was not sure how much lower my self-esteem
could go. But it has also been exceedingly rewarding as I stumbled upon
new paths to convert each disappointment into an opportunity to grow
and become more confident in who I was. Sometimes, that has meant
becoming overzealous in my own self-affirmation, the tone of my voice
taking on a sharper edge as I explained to others why pride in Blackness
was a requisite characteristic of any kind of Black progress. But I justify
that stridence by thinking of the dearth of encouragement from sources
that are not bothered by the profundity of Blackness—including the educational system, popular culture, and mainstream media.

The bitterness that comes with the construction of race as a state of
being and the making of racism as a behavior and attitude can be tasted
potently in the New World. It takes a fundamental encounter with whiteness for one to truly appreciate the meaning of Blackness. However, a picture of tribalism and ethnic tensions is vividly displayed in the midst of

Race and the American Story. Stephanie Shonekan and Adam Seagrave, Oxford University Press.
© Oxford University Press 2024. DOI: 10.1093/oso/9780197767689.003.0002

Blackness, in the heart of Africa. So my story has been a two-pronged journey through tribalism and racism.

A couple of years ago, my Trinidadian mother told me about an episode from my childhood that I had conveniently and completely forgotten. Apparently, one day my mother's close friend, Miss Tovson, came to visit. Miss T, as she was affectionately called, was one of several Americans who were active in my mother's expatriate community in Jos, Nigeria, during the 1970s and 1980s. Without exception, all the American missionaries that we knew then were white. It never even occurred to me to wonder why there were no African American missionaries. In any case, I was only six or seven years old when this particular episode took place, so I have tried to cut myself some slack for the horrific implications of this story. My mother says that I disappeared during Miss T's visit and when they came looking for me, they found me in the bathroom carefully scrubbing away at my arm with a wet tissue. I can only imagine the two women's expressions when they saw this little girl hard at work and determined to achieve something impossible.

"What are you doing?" my mother asked.

"I want to look like her," the little girl replied, briefly pointing at Miss T, the white American who looked like most of the other fortunate little girls in her missionary school, and continued the insurmountable task of rubbing away the dark layer of skin. Since her head was turned away from the two women, the girl did not see the expressions that must have passed over their faces. Was it pity, amusement, resignation, or horror?

Today, I think about that story and want nothing more than to say that I don't recognize that little girl. I would like to say that she is not someone I could ever relate to. But that would be untrue. I recognize her as myself, but also as so many other Black girls I have met in West Africa and in the Americas, who have all tried to rub away that oppressive coat of cultural and physical Blackness and gain acceptance in a world that has convinced them that they can never be beautiful or acceptable as long as their skin falls within the color spectrum from chocolate to coffee. I remember moments of deep sadness in my teenage years in Nigeria when I would stare at the mirror and wish that my features were less pronounced and that my skin was at least several shades lighter. We all knew that the biracial girls got a lot more attention from the guys than the darker skinned girls. And when I would sit and listen to my Trinidadian mother and her peers, I would hear descriptions of pretty "brown-skinned" girls and I would pray to God that I could get slightly lighter.

As I think about this, another memory disturbs me. Perhaps I was about ten or eleven when I went to bed one night. As I silently said my prayers, I asked God earnestly to change my appearance. This was probably the first real test of my faith. I squeezed my eyes shut and presented to God most sincerely the deepest desire of my heart. That my skin would be lighter when I woke up, and that my features would be changed dramatically. I truly believed that my prayer had been heard and the angels had been dispatched to put things in order. When I woke up the following morning, I rushed to the mirror and found the same dark girl staring me down. I was heartbroken. I have never told anyone this story. I had forgotten about it.

Today I am a professor of Black studies and music. I proudly walk the campus in my dark brown skin, teaching classes that nudge students to think about the value of race and the profundity of Blackness. I remember coming across this phrase—"the profundity of Blackness"—when I was myself a young impressionable undergraduate student in Nigeria. It appeared in the work of Claude McKay as he led the Black literati during the Harlem Renaissance. I thought a lot about how vast and complex the cloak of Blackness was, and how each angle gives you a different perspective. With my mother from one part of the Black world and my father from a different part, I knew that there were deep differences. The way my mother cooks greens or okra is different from how my father cooks them.

Today, when my students consider the expressive cultures of the Black world, we consider the implications of African heritage and ethnicity. A play by Wole Soyinka or August Wilson, a short story by Ngugi wa Thiong'o or Derek Walcott, a poem by Nikki Giovanni or Langston Hughes, or a song by Nina Simone or Fela Anikulapo Kuti—all these lend us opportunities to delve into the issues of identity that take us on a journey to Blackness. As I listen to students, Black and otherwise, tentatively venture into these discussions and try out theories that they have been encouraged to avoid and ignore throughout their lives and academic careers, I feel that I am having an impact on their lives. It is important for Black students to deliberate on themselves and the legacies that brought them to this classroom; but it is equally important for other students—non-Black students—to see that Black people have depth and history and culture. It is important for both groups to know that so many Black people have risen above the place where society has consciously and unconsciously tried to leave them. But most importantly, it is important for all students of life to understand how whiteness shaped and constructed Blackness, whether in Africa or the diaspora.

So when my mother told me the story of that little girl trying to wipe away her Blackness, I was shocked. And when I remembered the prayer of my twelve-year-old self, I almost wept. I did not have the full picture. I wonder how I got from there to here, to a place where I would not even accept one drop of milk in this particular dark chocolate complexion of mine.

Two dolls had a significant impact on my childhood thoughts about race. Their names were Ingrid and Diana. The first doll I remember truly treasuring was called Ingrid. She had very pale skin, blue eyes, a smattering of freckles over a tiny nose, pink lips, and silky brown hair. I adored Ingrid. I loved stroking her hair, so unlike my own thick, full cloud of Black hair. I don't remember how long I had Ingrid but she is a permanent memory of my childhood. I remember that her hair started getting matted and dull, so she was with me for a good while. There is a photo of me at my fifth birthday party, holding on to Ingrid, while cutting into my magnificent birthday cake, which was a doll cake, a gorgeous confection built around a white barbie. I now wonder what must have seeped into my mind, and the minds of all my Nigerian girl guests, about the contrasts in our identities, and if the episode with Miss T and the scrubbing of my skin had anything to do with thoughts that had lived so comfortably in my consciousness.

When I was about ten years old, after Ingrid was long gone, my beautiful mother bought me a new doll for my birthday. It was a barbie doll—a

fabulous Diana Ross Barbie doll! I cannot properly express my utter de-
light in this gift. I did not want to open the package. I just wanted to gaze at
Diana through the plastic front of the box. She was tall, slender, busty (of
course), and brown. Just a few shades lighter than me. And her hair! It was
full, big, still silky, but also textured. I adored that doll. She looked like her
inspiration on the Supremes' album covers, and on her solo albums. I have
vivid memories of the *The Boss* album cover. She stands there, a gorgeous
Black woman, with big textured hair, in a green and gray casual outfit,
staring unabashedly at the camera. We played that album again and again
on the record player in the living room. When I got the Diana doll, I forgot
all about Ingrid because there was something so heartwarming about a
doll that could have been one of my own family.[1] I didn't quite get the intricate meanings of the contrasts between these two dolls, but looking back
on Ingrid and Diana, I know that my young mind was forming questions,
reaching shaky conclusions about who I was and what the world would
look like for me.

Around this time, Nigeria hosted a pan-African arts festival called
FESTAC '77.[2] That festival, hosted in Lagos, was televised, and folks all
over the country watched the performances for days. So, even though I was
in Jos, in the middle of the country, I felt as though I attended FESTAC.
The festival was truly unprecedented. Never before had a group of Black
artists from around the world been brought together in one place, at one
time, to present the beauty of African and African diasporan art: theater,
music, and dance. I was completely mesmerized by the exuberance of Ipi
Tombi, a dance ensemble from South Africa who hit the stage with gorgeous women, moving gracefully to the drums of the Zulu and the Xhosa;
I absorbed the joy of Stevie Wonder, who sat at his keyboard, in his da-
shiki and cornrows, and serenaded a stadium full of the Lagos community; I was bewildered and intrigued by the moves and message of James
Brown when he executed remarkable dance moves on that FESTAC stage
with "Say It Loud, I'm Black and I'm Proud!"; and when Mighty Sparrow
took the stage, my mother sang along to all her favorite calypso songs,

which were so familiar to me because we had all his records at home. To say that this festival made an impression on me would be an understatement. Imagine a young Black girl nine or ten years old, watching this vast display of Black excellence! Something deep within me was sparked, although that fascination with the profundity of Blackness would stay quietly smoldering for many years to come.

The question I often ask myself is why it takes so long for these revelations to reach us. Why does the smoldering take so long? Adam and I, growing up in different countries and circumstances across the world, both tarried with seeing the clear and full picture. For me, being raised in a former colony meant that I was still deeply entangled with the murky aftermath of colonialism. The streams of the empire had been drained, but it left behind the pesky residuals of Western identity. We can pick out these particles— standards of beauty, aesthetics of art, systems of education, canons of knowledge, modes of democracy. But there is one remnant that trumps the others—religion. Interestingly, both Adam and I were raised Catholic—he in California, and I in Nigeria. From as early as I can remember, my mother took us to mass every Sunday. We had a beloved Irish priest—Father Mason—who was almost part of the family. My siblings and I had our own missals, went through the rites of passage—first Holy Communion and Confirmation. We were all married in the Catholic church.

Thousands of miles, cultures, and oceans away, Adam went through the same rites of passage. Faith is a fundamental thing. It provides a lens through which to see the world and a set of instructions for navigating life. It sits at the very core of your being, whispering directions on how to see and treat others and how to see oneself. It is the first thing one taps into when one is confused or in trouble. In many ways, religious faith is ephemeral—there is nothing really solid or stable about it, but once latched onto, it becomes an almost immovable foundation on which people base their most fundamental beliefs about themselves and about the world. Throughout world history, faith has caused the most horrific events and the most compassionate interventions that have affected millions of people across many generations. On a macro level, religious faith has led to bloody crusades and terrible fundamentalisms. It has also pushed for social change and equality.

This schizophrenic nature of faith makes it a complicated phenomenon at the micro/personal level. As children, Adam and I were introduced to the same tenets of the Catholic faith. We both attended mass, learned the order of service, knew when to stand, kneel, genuflect, and make the proper sign of the cross. At the most granular level, we were given images and stories to set the standard of our faith and to provide answers to our young minds. Perhaps the biggest image introduced to us in our different worlds was the image of Jesus Christ himself. As I look back at the beginning of our faith, I have to wonder why we were offered the same image of Jesus. I grew up with a blond-haired, blue-eyed Jesus—one who had the same skin tone as Adam (not the one in Eden, the one I'm writing this book with!). This Jesus was illustrated on the pages of my missal, he was on our Christmas cards and on the walls of our church in Jos, Nigeria. As a little Black Catholic girl, I regarded this image as the very definition of God. And yet, we were taught in our catechism classes that man is made in the image of God. So what does it mean to a young mind to regard the image of a God as someone who looks nothing like her or her people? How does this distortion set into her worldview? If God is white, and the colonizers were white, and the slavers were white, what is the level of her own psyche and self-esteem? How does this complicated awareness of self through faith differ from the one formed in the minds of other children around the world? And what happened to the image of God that our ancestors had before we were colonized and enslaved?

Unconsciously, these questions of faith follow us into adulthood and remain with us today. Grappling with these contradictions and ironies of faith, no matter what the religion is, is an important part of our evolution to racial justice and freedom. Adam and I are both still people of faith, but our journeys to this point could not have been more distinct.

* * *

THE COLORBLINDSPOT

I grew up in a very white world. I got into Stanford simply by birth—and by that I mean I was born in the Stanford University Hospital—and then moved to Napa, California, from the South Bay Area when I was eight. During the first years of my life, we lived in nice-sounding places like Sunnyvale and Mountain View. Having begun life at a prestigious university, I spent my childhood in sunny vales with views of mountains before transitioning to vineyards and wineries. We had moved to Napa primarily for the sake of a very small private Catholic school there, which I attended through eighth grade. Clearly, I was privileged.

Personal stories are never this simple, however, and my childhood was no exception. Money was always very tight. My father left when I was thirteen, forcing my mother to work two jobs while my three siblings and I largely shifted for ourselves. None of us had any personal connections or financial assistance to draw on as we went out into the world and applied to colleges and jobs. Growing up around incredible affluence, we had very little.

I can count on one hand the number of people I knew throughout my childhood who might be identified as Black. I had no racist feelings or tendencies whatsoever. I couldn't, really, because I didn't have any feelings or thoughts about nonwhite people at all. I didn't care either way, and I didn't know any better. I was, in a way, "colorblind" because I literally never saw anyone of a different color; or, if I did, I merely saw them without *seeing* them. I was spared the internal agony of feeling different, or worse, because of my skin color; and it wasn't until hearing Stephanie's heart-wrenching childhood story of trying to wash away her appearance that I realized the enormity of my personal blindness about the experiences associated with skin color. We all have our challenges and hardships, of course, and some of us more than others; but not all of us have had the experience of trying to feel comfortable in our own skin when it is that very skin that seems to be standing in the way. Empathy dictates that we listen to and learn from those who have had that experience. I, like most white

Americans, had never made the effort to exercise that kind of empathy. My colorblindness was a moral blindness.

Now, two decades later, I'm codirecting a national project on race in American society. I've arrived at a conviction that African Americans' struggle for justice is the central, defining case for understanding the importance of the American experiment. I've realized that repairing the racial divide in the United States is not a utopian cliché but the most urgent and necessary goal for perpetuating the American democratic republic. Most importantly, I've come to the conclusion that people like me need to really care about Black Americans. Not simply care about social justice, or diversity, or economic inequality, or inclusion, or some other vague abstraction; but care about actual Black people, truly seeing and appreciating the humanity that shines with equal force through every individual human being of every color, shape, and size like sunlight through a window.

My own story as it relates to race and the American story is about how I got from there to here. If I got here, maybe others can as well.

Part of the reason I was able to remain completely oblivious to issues of racial justice in the United States for so long was that I grew up before the twenty-four-hour news and entertainment cycle brought about by digital and social media. Most American kids in the 1980s and early 1990s simply weren't often exposed to images or news of any kind from the world beyond their local communities and personal acquaintances. I remember, for example, joining a group of students around a car radio to listen to the reading of the verdict in the O.J. Simpson trial when I was thirteen. I had no opinion regarding the case, and had joined the group simply out of curiosity. When the verdict had been read, I went back to playing basketball and didn't give it any further thought. I didn't know anything about Rodney King or the Los Angeles riots until college, or even later. It wasn't that I was opposed to the progress of racial justice, or that I dismissed the importance of what happened to Rodney King, or that I denied the wider significance of race-infused police brutality—it simply didn't register on the radar screen of my consciousness, like a dust storm on Mars or the birth of a baby panda in China.

I spent a significant portion of my childhood playing classical music—the piano and the cello. My parents were both piano teachers and we owned a music store in Napa. When I was a baby we lived for about a year in Austria while my parents studied piano performance. I frequently participated in competitions and attended workshops until my high school years (when I insisted on shifting my priorities to sports). These events—and even my regular weekly lessons in San Francisco—took me far from Napa, to places with more diverse populations. I met dozens, hundreds of fellow musicians from around the country. I can still see many of their faces—mostly white, many Asian, some Indian. I don't remember seeing a single Black classical musician.

Of course I didn't think anything of this at the time, but this memory—or, in this case, lack of a memory—came rushing back to me during an event we hosted a few years ago on Race and American Music. Stephanie was, at the time, a professor in the Music Department at Mizzou. During this event, she was engaging in conversation with a former student of hers at Mizzou, a very talented singer. While they were talking, there was mention in passing of the fact that Black students are treated very differently in music departments; they are informally but definitely segregated into the study of certain genres and instruments. They are routinely excluded, in particular, from classical forms of musical expression.[3] Now this is old news to many, and was far from a surprise to me. But it was the first time I had consciously made sense of my own childhood experience in the classical music world.

Music is an important part of the Race and the American Story course and project. It is a vitally important component of Black American experience and identity. One of the best articles in the *New York Times* "1619 Project" focuses on this importance, and on the enormous contributions of Black Americans to American music in general. According to the very erudite, Harvard-educated W. E. B. Du Bois in *The Souls of Black Folk*, the "Sorrow Songs" of enslaved African Americans represented "the sole American music," "the most beautiful expression of human experience born this side the seas," and "the singular spiritual heritage of the nation."[4] And yet, growing up steeped in musical culture in the United States, and from an extended family occupied with musical pursuits to an extreme degree, I knew nothing about Black American music and had never met a Black American who played either of my instruments.

This blind spot with respect to issues of race in the United States—this "colorblindspot"—also extended to American history. Though I'm sure we read about Martin Luther King Jr. and the civil rights movement in grade school and high school, the emphasis was so insignificant that I have no recollection of having ever done so.[5] I knew vaguely that the enslavement of African Americans had happened, and that it was now over, but that was roughly the extent of my knowledge. Nothing about the transatlantic slave trade or the horrors of lynching in the post-Reconstruction South, much less about the positive contributions of African Americans to American life. Frederick Douglass, Harriett Tubman, Sojourner Truth, Ida Wells, Frances Harper, Anna Julia Cooper, W. E. B. DuBois, Malcolm X, were all completely unknown to me until long after high school.[6] As far as I and the kids I grew up with were concerned, African Americans were enslaved and now they're not, and that's all anyone needs to know about African American history.

This ability to make it through childhood—and even, for many, adult life—without ever having to worry about or grapple with instances of racism or unjust disadvantage is one manifestation of what is often referred to as "white privilege." This term was popularized in the late 1980s—around the time I moved to Napa—but builds on the penetrating psychological analysis of W. E. B. DuBois in the early twentieth century. The things to which the term "white privilege" refers, some of which are contained in the forty-six-point list Peggy McIntosh compiled in her seminal article on the topic, are certainly real. The experience of my childhood and that of innumerable others clearly attests to this. People who look white are simply exempted from all sorts of concerns, hurdles, and obstacles that constantly and necessarily impose themselves on people of color; and, in the context of the United States, on people of African descent in particular. My childhood action figures, unlike Stephanie's first doll, all looked more or less like me.

I've come to think, though, that speaking of these exemptions in terms of "privilege" is both unhelpful and misleading. It is unhelpful because it immediately angers and alienates most of the people who need to be persuaded to change their minds if the phenomena to which "white privilege" refers are ever to be rectified. White Americans who are wealthy usually want to believe that their wealth and social status is the result of merit or hard work, not unearned privilege. White Americans who are poor have difficulty seeing themselves as privileged in any way.[7] The term seems to them an insensitive dismissal of the often-extreme hardships and challenges they have faced in their lives. Many white people in middle America and Appalachia were persuaded to become Trump voters precisely as a result of this perceived dismissal at the hands of progressive liberal culture. Most white people in modern America face severe tragedy and difficulty at various points throughout their lives; to label such people "privileged" jars badly with their experience of life.

"White privilege" is misleading because it mischaracterizes the struggle for racial justice as jockeying for social position rather than a fight for rights. The problem with slavery was not that white slaveholders enjoyed the "privilege" of being able to sit on their porches and drink mint juleps all day. The real problem was that African American slaves were deprived of their basic natural rights to liberty, property, and the pursuit of happiness. The problem with Jim Crow laws and segregation was not that white people got to vote, hold political office, freely use public facilities, and live their lives under the protection of the law. That was all well and good. The real problem was that formerly enslaved African Americans were unjustly deprived of the right to vote and hold political office, unjustly degraded by being systematically excluded from public places, and unjustly deprived of the equal protection of the law. The problem with ongoing issues of systemic racial economic inequality, systemic racial inequality in educational opportunities, and systemic racial disparities in the enforcement of criminal justice is not that white people are systematically handed wealth, education, and get-out-of-jail-free cards; it is that African Americans are unjustly deprived of equal economic and educational opportunities, and are unjustly targeted by laws and enforcement practices that should be protecting them.[8]

You get the point. America's problem with race has never been that white people get to live normally. It has always been that nonwhite people and other marginalized groups have been treated unjustly and excluded from doing the same. The good and important process of bringing white people to an awareness of the vast disparities between their experience of day to day life in America and that of Black Americans should not be billed as a consciousness of privilege, but as a consciousness of systemic and historically path-dependent injustice. The problem is not privilege but apathy in the face of injustice. The problem is that white Americans tend to go about their lives as if they live on an island apart from people unlike them. And as blissfully oblivious islanders, they fail to see their own lives and times as only the visible peaks of mountains extending into unplumbed depths beneath them. The opposite of injustice is not privilege, but justice. The opposite of apathy is not self-awareness, but altruism.

I hear some of my readers saying at this point—What difference does it make? Isn't white privilege the same thing as Black disadvantage? In my classes we talk a lot about both, and the conversations that students have about each are completely different. The white privilege conversation usually goes something like this:

John: I was driving in a car once with a friend who was Black, and a cop asked for his ID but didn't ask for mine. That was when I realized how privileged I am because I am white.
[rest of class nods their heads silently]

The Black disadvantage conversation, on the other hand, goes more like this:

John: I was driving in a car once with a friend who was Black, and a cop asked for his ID but didn't ask for mine. I asked the cop why he didn't need to see my ID, and he gave a reason that didn't sound convincing

to me. I called the police department later and complained that this
was unfair to my friend.

Jane: This reminds me of the problem of racial disparities in rates of
incarceration and the role of the criminal justice system in enforcing
racial hierarchy in the Jim Crow South after the Civil War. Is this just
a way in which this same old problem is rearing its head today?

In both cases, the starting point is the same: a problematic manifestation of racial hierarchy. When this problem is addressed in terms of
white privilege, three results emerge: (1) an expression of (normally quite
self-congratulatory) guilt on the part of white people—"that was when
I realized how privileged I am because I am white"; (2) a silence signifying
agreement by some and a fear to disagree by the rest—the nodding heads;
and (3) inaction. When the problem is addressed in terms of Black disadvantage or injustice, on the other hand, three quite different results
emerge: (1) an immediate concern for obtaining equal justice for others—
"I asked the cop why he didn't need to see my ID. . . . I called the police department and complained"; (2) an openness to continuing the discussion
along productive lines, such as exploring the background conditions and
history of the current situation—Jane's insightful comment; and (3) an
awareness of a clear problem that has a (relatively) clear solution to which
we can contribute.

The phrase "white privilege" might make a lot of sense from the perspective of nonwhite people, but its effect on white people is only to encourage their self-absorption. It provides a way for white people to be
"good" in a very easy and comfortable way, without ever looking beyond
themselves or reaching outside of their comfort zones to others. I can be
aware of my white privilege all by myself; I can wallow in pleasant feelings
of acknowledged guilt; I can be congratulated by others for my mere self-
awareness; and all the while I never have to worry about helping anyone
else, or fighting for racial justice in my community. Shift from the perspective of privilege to the perspective of injustice, and all of a sudden
we have to *do* something. We have to do something in collaboration and

dialogue with others, and we have to effect change in the world through our joint action.

The problem with white privilege isn't that white people are privileged, it is that we are on an island that is safe not only from injustice, but from the motivation to care about the injustice done to others elsewhere. Martin Luther King Jr. once said that "injustice anywhere is a threat to justice everywhere." White American islanders might admire this quotation when it is etched on a memorial in Washington, DC, but we are safe from having to actually take it seriously. This isn't privilege; it is psychological insularity from injustices that aren't done to people like us. It is a universal characteristic of human nature—self-centeredness—that can only be overcome through radical and forceful counteraction. White privilege is really white insularity: the ability to live on an island where racial injustice doesn't happen and doesn't matter.

White insularity is itself the result of racism, or at least preracist tendencies to form social circles and communities that exclude people who are very different from oneself. In the United States, these natural tendencies have historically been magnified by the social construction of racial stereotypes. For generations, having African ancestry in the United States was reliably associated with the status of being enslaved. After the abolition of slavery, having African American ancestry became socially associated with poverty, criminality, and a particular cultural identity alien to that of white Americans. In response to these racist stereotypes in combination with preracist human tendencies, white Americans have built intricate social archipelagos that generally exclude Black Americans. These archipelagos then lead to exclusionary systems and practices resulting in disadvantages—and, indeed, injustices—to Black Americans.

This forms a part of what Stephanie and Tomiwa encountered upon coming to the United States. In their case, these racist and preracist social dynamics were complicated by the fact that they did not have African American ancestry. They initially seemed, in Stephanie's terms, to be more "comfortable" or "safe" Black folks to be around for white Americans since they were relative outsiders to African American history—Africans, not African Americans. This complicating outsider status, however, did not exempt them from experiencing the terrible racism that has protected many white American islands like jagged seaside cliffs. White islands exist throughout the United States, and they support and sustain the disadvantages, exclusions, and injustices that Black Americans too often suffer as a result of their racial identity.

Tragedy and personal struggle in general, on the other hand, know no race. The experience of parental abandonment as a child, particularly during the formative psychological period of early adolescence, was a significant hurdle for me to overcome. In my case, as in most similar cases, the loss of one parent really meant the substantial loss of both; the remaining parent is left with the practical and emotional fallout of the loss, which significantly reduces the amount of time and energy available to devote to children. My mother heroically kept the lights on, providing an example of dedication and, most importantly, passing on the religious faith that has been my constant guide through life. ·

In so many immediate practical and developmental ways, though, I was left with a steeply uphill struggle. No one ever taught me how to shave, tie a tie, or barbecue. No one ever gave me advice on how to get a job, how to build and maintain relationships, or how to deal with defeat and disappointment. I had to figure all of that out, or not figure it out, on my own (I still probably shave wrong, though I've gotten pretty good with a grill). In college I would dropkick the basketball a hundred feet in the air after nearly every loss, and often after disappointing plays within a game. I was often dangerously close to the wrong side of the law, and if I had gotten there I might have stayed there for good. Looking back, I'm still puzzled as to how my girlfriend (now wife) stuck with me through those difficult periods of delayed maturation and belated self-parenting.

This is an all-too-common experience for the millions of children who grow up in single-parent families, or without any family structure at all. The tragic loss or persistent absence of parents, family members, and friends is a human experience that unites people of every race, ethnicity, national background, or other form of personal identity. Thirty-four percent of children in the United States lived in single-parent families in 2017.[9] Seventy-eight percent of kids ages eleven to sixteen reported that at least one of their close friends or relatives had died. Seven in ten teachers report currently having at least one student in their class who has lost a parent, guardian, sibling, or close friend in the past year.[10] Tragedy, loss, and absence are human events that nearly everyone experiences at some point in their lives, and that many experience in the formative and delicate period of childhood. Americans of every description are disadvantaged, or underprivileged, in these important ways.

These types of human events are not, though, equally shared by all segments of American society. White Americans and African Americans occupy the two extremes on nearly every measure. In 2017, 24 percent of white American children were growing up, as I did, in single-parent families; that number was 65 percent for African American children.[11] African Americans are about three times more likely to have experienced the death of an immediate family member before age thirty than are white Americans.[12] A recent study by the CDC found that there has been remarkable persistence in a particularly depressing statistical disparity: infants of Black mothers in the United States have a mortality rate more than two times that of white, Asian, or Hispanic mothers.[13]

These statistics reveal a wide gap between white and African Americans in terms of their aggregate experiences of life (and death) in American society. In another way, though, these statistics also provide a basis for the forging of common bonds through empathy. One thing we all share clearly as human beings is the experience of tragedy and loss. These experiences can and should provide a foundation for empathy, which can in turn serve as a basis for further mutual understanding. I experienced the early loss of a parent as a child, and I have experienced the loss of a child as a parent. These experiences have led me to care deeply about those beyond my white island who have had similarly tragic life experiences. And this caring is the first step toward addressing the problematic racial disparities along many dimensions of human life that are often labeled in terms of white privilege.

Cicero wrote that nothing in the world is so like something else as one human being is like another.[14] Frederick Douglass wrote that he saw himself as a human being first, and a Black American second.[15] This kind of abstract perspective can be viewed as itself a manifestation of white privilege: people are in a way enabled to identify more with humanity in general if they aren't painfully reminded of their more particular identities through frequent injustice or pervasive oppression (the extraordinary example of Frederick Douglass notwithstanding).

In my own experience this certainly rings true. A radio host once introduced me to his listeners as someone who identified as white.[16] My immediate reaction was first to laugh—thinking it might be a joke—and then to deny its accuracy. I don't identify as a white human being, but simply as a human being. Now, I'm as white as all of my least favorite condiments. But most white people don't "identify" as white in any sort of active or conscious sense. No one had ever treated me as a *white* person or even referred to me in those terms; I was just a person. I have never felt the way Stephanie has with respect to racial identity; like owning and celebrating it in order to transform racial identity from a weapon of oppression into a source of strength.

This certainly has something to do with the fact that Americans of European ancestry—"white" people—have always constituted a majority of American society. Such people have not experienced any targeted exclusion, injustice, or oppression because of their racial identity (nationality is a different story, but this is a story for another time). In the American republic we believe in the rule of law—in the idea that the law applies equally to all citizens regardless of their distinguishing characteristics or other status. Think of lady justice with the blindfold and the scale. This ideal has enabled those who are in fact treated equally to abstract from their particular distinguishing identities. My equal treatment under the law has made the color of my skin irrelevant to me.

The statement that "all men are created equal" in the Declaration of Independence has a similar effect. Just as everyone who is treated equally under the law is able to think of themselves as "citizen," so everyone whose natural human rights are respected and protected is able to think of themselves as "man." The way I see it, this isn't the conferring of privileged status but the removal of what W. E. B. Du Bois referred to as a "veil."[17] Being human isn't a privilege; it's a condition. But at least it's a natural and inescapable—and, therefore, just—condition. It isn't the result of one part of humanity imposing its selfish will on another part.

One of the ways in which Cicero thought all humans were so alike was in our capacity to act in ways below our humanity. This capacity is really a tendency. One of the worst manifestations of the human condition is the tendency to try and reduce other human beings to a level below this condition. Looking down on others gives us the optical illusion of being higher up than we actually are.

Because this is really a universal feature of humanity, though, the fact is that no one's racial, ethnic, or national identity will forever render them immune to oppression. What goes around inevitably comes around. If we want our children, grandchildren, great-great-great grandchildren to be able to identify with their humanity, we should try to be more human our-selves. We should fight the tendency to attempt to escape the negativity of the human condition by placing ourselves above others. The human condition is inescapable, and a clear recognition of this fact has the power to inspire great sympathy and caring between humans separated by im-mense distance and time.

Two Experiences, One Nation

GETTING EDUCATED, WAKING UP

I began by saying I did not know I was Black until I came to the United States. What I mean is that my understanding of the fullness of that concept became more pronounced when I moved to the United States for graduate school. As a child growing up in the postcolonial sub-Saharan country of Nigeria, I was aware of my Blackness as a sort of subhuman quality, but I was not constantly reminded of that fact. When my siblings and I attended a predominantly white American Lutheran missionary k–12 school in Nigeria, I grappled with the color hierarchy that was instilled in the society, which, to be honest, had been there since the British presence in the country. Something about the experience of attending school with these white kids, most of whom did not care to interact with local Nigerians outside the school, did not sit right with me. So, when I reached fifth grade and my mother gave me a choice to continue there or attend a local Nigerian secondary school, I bravely chose the latter. I spent the next five years among native Nigerians, and the oppressive clouds of European hegemony hovered only through our curriculum—the literary and historical texts were British; the structure of our educational system was patterned along the lines of the British system; our religious services included Catholic mass and protestant services (there was no room for African traditional religious beliefs); and so on. Looking back, I know now that this was just another manifestation of European supremacy.[1] Thinking back

Race and the American Story. Stephanie Shonekan and Adam Seagrave, Oxford University Press.
© Oxford University Press 2024. DOI: 10.1093/oso/9780197767689.003.0003

to our literature classes, I can remember *The Mayor of Casterbridge, Julius Caesar, Merchant of Venice, Moll Flanders*, and so many other samples drawn from the so-called canon. I know we read Achebe's *No Longer at Ease* and *Things Fall Apart*, but that was a drop in the ocean of British literature. All our science, geography, and history text books were written by Europeans. And what is alarming about this is that I went to secondary school more than twenty years after independence from Britain. This means that even when the Union Jack came down on October 1, 1960, its influence was already so deeply rooted, it was as if its phantom continued to flutter in the wind, overshadowing the entire country with its power.

I have early whitewashed memories of my middle-class upbringing: my father, who eschewed his Igbo names for his English or Christian name, Steven; wearing his suits, puffing from his pipes, the smell of tobacco filling the entire house, the sound of Frank Sinatra and Perry Como filtering through the speakers of the gramophone player. I recall Saturdays spent at the exclusive golf club, since my father was an avid golfer, ordering club sandwiches and chapman drinks from the waitstaff dressed in stiff white uniforms. This club had mostly white members, with a sprinkling of Nigerian members, the lucky few who had been trained in England, had good government jobs, and knew how to perform whiteness to the point that made the white members feel comfortable and at home, thousands of miles from England.

This is not unique to Nigeria. The same is true in Trinidad, where my mother is from. All former colonies had this same relationship with the empires of which they were a part. It was like a bad breakup, the kind where one partner is so obsessed with the former lover that they keep going back, obsessing over and yearning for all the bad behavior that led to the breakup in the first place. There is always an imbalance in this relationship. The abuser always has the upper hand, which holds the keys to the handcuffs that are still attached virtually and tightly. The abuse is visible in our names, our clothes, our types of recreation, the football clubs we support and cheer for (read Premier League!), and so on. If one is unconvinced of the endurance of this relationship, one has only to ask a few questions: how many Europeans bear African names, cheer for African football clubs, know of the African traditional gods, sing African folk songs. And the questions go on and on. This imbalance is a result of white supremacy. What we have in the United States is a particular distilled, ugly version of a global problem.

I think there is much to be said about Black consciousness in the United States and how that has helped me to find beauty and comfort in my dark-skinned self. Growing up in Nigeria, Blackness was like a light cloak that was thrown over me when I was among white folks or when we watched television, or read about the most beautiful people in *People* magazine. This cloak would easily slide off once I was in the community, among the majority population of Black folks. When I moved to the United States, that cloak of Blackness became a heavier, permanent part of my being because of the history of race in the United States. I had read about this history. The first time I truly considered racism was when *Roots* was shown on our television in Nigeria. We watched the miniseries as a family and were horrified by the story and the deeper implications of what had happened to Africans who had been transported across the Atlantic in the seventeenth and eighteenth centuries. Although my mother, having been born and raised in Trinidad, had ancestors who made that journey, she had never talked about this. Even when I watched *Roots*, it never occurred to me that I had an ancestor who had been captured somewhere along the coast of West Africa, loaded on a ship, endured the horrific months of the middle passage, and offloaded like cargo in the West Indies. I remember the pain and sadness the moment that Kunta Kinte's foot was chopped off for trying to escape enslavement, I remember the pride I felt when he refused to accept his slave name "Toby." But I also remember the sharp needling of confusion over the thought that my own name was Stephanie, clearly not a Nigerian traditional name. What does it mean that I bear an English name? Why is English our national language? Why do we ladies straighten our hair? Why do some women lighten their skin with skin-bleaching cream? Why do African men seem to prefer lighter skinned women? Why did we read Shakespeare's *Julius Caesar* and Thomas Hardy's *The Mayor of Casterbridge* before we encountered Nigerian authors like Chinua Achebe or Wole Soyinka? As I think about all these questions, it is clear that the history of colonization in Africa is tightly interwoven in the fabric of racism. At the root of all my questions is the notion that the pride and personhood of Black people were stamped out by white Europeans. What we have as the manifestation of racism in the United States draws from the same fount of imperial racism enacted by the British Empire.

Although I did not move to the United States until 1996, I began to get a clearer picture of the complexities of racism when I was an English major at the University of Jos in Nigeria in the 1980s. I threw myself into African literature and found myself empathizing with characters like Okonkwo in Achebe's *Things Fall Apart*, and Kamau in Ngugi's *Weep Not Child*. These characters struggled with the conditions resulting from the clash of unequal cultures. When the white folks arrived and settled, both Okonkwo in Nigeria and Kamau in Kenya knew that this intrusion would have a fatal effect on the agency, property, sanctity, and integrity of African tradition and identity.

Then I enrolled in a class titled Literature of the African Diaspora, which blew my mind. At last, all the questions I had growing up began to be answered. When I read Caribbean novels and poetry (George Lamming, Edgar Mittelholzer, Derek Walcott) and African American literature (James Baldwin, Richard Wright, Toni Morrison), I saw connections to what I was learning in African literature. The book that made the most striking impact was Ralph Ellison's *Invisible Man*. In the prologue, Ellison's character states, "I am an invisible man.... That invisibility to which I refer occurs because of a peculiar disposition of the eyes of those with whom I come into contact. A matter of construction of their *inner* eyes, those eyes with which they look through their physical eyes upon reality."[2] As I followed that character and his struggles, I began to see race and power emerge as a unifying theme.

I remember reading that and connecting this protagonist to Okonkwo and Kamau. The dots began to connect for me. I could understand my mother's people and my father's people so much better now. My senior thesis was on the race and class distinctions in Trinidadian writer Edgar Mittelholzer's *A Day at the Office*. This book opened up a world of understanding for me, as Mittelholzer presents the prejudices that are embedded in the interactions between fourteen ordinary characters who work at an ordinary office. My emerging scholarly mind took in the social hierarchy built on the shades of skin color from darkest at the bottom to lightest at the top, and found resonance in what I was experiencing at home in Nigeria. This rich, slim novel, along with the other books I read in my African Diaspora Literature course, confirmed the deep and far-reaching roots of racism and its effects internally on the nonwhite community in the form of colorism.

I continued this exploration during my master's degree at the University of Ibadan. This time, I wanted to focus my attentions squarely on African American experiences through the writing of Langston Hughes and Leroi Jones/Amiri Baraka and the music of Louis Armstrong and Miles Davis. I heard the cadences of the poetry, the timbre of the trumpets, the content of the struggle and insistence on freedom in these beautiful expressions of Black life. I explored the connections across artistic expressions and arrived at conclusions that pulled together the Black worlds that I had been exploring throughout my college career. Somewhere along this journey, between undergraduate and graduate degrees, I had been introduced to the music of Fela Anikulapo-Kuti.

A master of storytelling, political criticism, and stinging social commentary, Fela put a musical magnifying glass on the problems left over by white supremacy.[3] In every song he asks what we have become as a result of the interruption of our history. In "Lady" (1972) and "Colonial Mentality" (1980), he points to the psychological impact of colonialism, and to the resulting erosion of local and traditional ways of thinking and being. Another way of thinking about the ravishing of the African psyche by colonialism is stated by Audre Lorde in a speech: "For we must move against not only those forces which dehumanize us from the outside, but also against those oppressive values which we have been forced to take into ourselves."[4]

Fela raises the question of what happens to people who have been physically freed but have remained bound in other ways. These questions can be applied throughout the African diaspora, and Fela does this directly in his 1989 album *Beasts of No Nation*, where he adopts a Pan-African lens to shed light on the ravages of white supremacy wielded by world powers symbolized by Ronald Reagan, Margaret Thatcher, and the United Nations, and impacting places like Lebanon, Soweto in South Africa, and Zaria and Ife in Nigeria.

Fela made me think carefully not only about the concept of Blackness but also about the symbolism of whiteness. I was able to look around me; to review my upbringing; to return to what I had been raised to think about myself and about my people, my ravished cultures and traditions; and to confirm to myself that my academic journey was the right one for me. Within Nigeria, during my undergraduate and master's journeys, I became more conscious of the sharp inequalities in the power dynamic; I responded to Langston Hughes's poetic deliberations about a "dream deferred"; I was moved by Miles Davis's radical turns in jazz. But most of that was theoretical. There was no amount of reading or listening or watching that would have prepared me for the version of Black identity and its intimidating presence to the white mainstream, for race and racism as it is manifested in the United States.

LEARNING ABOUT BLACKNESS AND WHITENESS

It is really important to emphasize that the concept of Blackness exists in the United States because of the concept of whiteness. In other words, Black assertion was a needed retaliation to white supremacy. Historian Studs Terkel recalled what historian John Hope Franklin said about Blackness and whiteness on the anniversary of the centennial celebration of the Statue of Liberty: "The Poles, the Jews, the Italians and the Irish could all get together in their hostility to the Blacks. It has become another aspect of the democratic creed. Being white in America made them feel equal to other whites, as long as the Black man was down below."[5] If white folks continue to look down on Black folks, if this is written into the very founding documents of this country, Black folks will continually respond with a reminder that they are equal to every other group, and that they matter.

In "Minstrelsy and the Construction of Race in America," Jason Lee explores the long-standing tradition of minstrelsy as a way for white America to define "Blackness":

> From the outset, minstrelsy unequivocally branded Black Americans as inferiors. Its content provided assurances of white common people's identity by emphasizing the "peculiarities" and inferiority of Black individuals. These assurances, it seems, could not have come at a better time for the white community, whose official confirmation of Black inferiority—institutionalized slavery—vanished with the victory of the Union forces during the Civil War. The "Negro peculiarities" highlighted in popular culture and in minstrel songs allowed for white audiences to laugh in relief at the idiotic, backward behavior of Black characters on stage whose "Blackness" represented a set of inherent traits that would never allow Blacks to rise above their second-rate place in society. Physical appearance, manners of speech, and cultural practices were all caricaturized to stress "difference" and lowliness. Grotesque exaggerations became reality as audiences desperately sought any type of proof that whiteness was superior to Blackness.[6]

Lee's overview of minstrelsy points to an enduring truth about the ways in which Blackness is ascribed to inferiority. This meaning placed on Blackness became apparent to me as soon as we arrived in the United States in 1996. I had visited the United States a few times previously, but nothing prepares you for the subtleties and harshness of racism in this American life.

The week we arrived, my husband, Tomiwa, went for a walk. As he was waiting to cross a road in Bloomington Indiana, a truck passed by and a man pushed his head out the passenger side, red faced, and shouted at him: "Nigger!" Tomiwa was bewildered. He could not understand the anger and vitriol that his very presence, his dark six-foot body produced in this white man that did not know him. We both knew the history and knew that racism lingered stubbornly in the United States. We just weren't expecting it to show up so loudly in our first week. That occurrence set the tone for us; it raised our antennas and kept us on the alert. This also made us acutely aware of our Blackness. We suddenly looked down at ourselves, and studied the tone of the skin we had lived so comfortably in up to this point, and realized that we were instantly marked as different. Since then, it has always baffled and infuriated me when African immigrants arrive and swagger around as if they don't also wear this cloak of Blackness. Some of them say things like "we are not like the *akata*,[7]" "we are not Black," "we are not like them." African Americans often reciprocate with derogatory names like "booty scratcher." But the red-faced man in the truck does not care whether you are a booty scratcher or an *akata*. He cares about the fact that you are walking around his imagined white world in your Black skin.

Within our first few weeks of arrival, we noticed something else about our Blackness. We realized that white people were as diverse as Black people, but the mark of our Blackness followed us everywhere. Quite different from red-face-man-in-the-truck were the white Americans we met in church and in other "nice" spaces. As soon as we would open our mouths, these nice white folks would realize we were Motherland Black folks and not indigenous Black folks. White church folks would become immediately more comfortable with our presence. We learned very quickly that if we were Black African, we were embraced in a sort of paternalistic and patronizing way. A nice couple immediately took us under their wing and invited us to their home for our first Thanksgiving. As we were leaving, they brought out bags of old clothes and gifted us with our first winter coats. There is really nothing wrong with second-hand clothes. I love thrift shops to this day. We were grateful for these things because we really had no money to buy them ourselves. So off we went with our bounty of second-hand stuff. As I look back on that Thanksgiving giftbag, I am reminded of how widely we smiled that day, of all the questions they asked us about "African life," and I am reflecting on how these nice-white folks stopped seeing us when we started pushing back gently against their stereotypes and when we began asking questions about the history of racism in this country. Gone were the invitations for meals at their homes. We were no longer comfortable Black folks.

Again and again over the years, I have canceled or been canceled by white church folks who love to extend their missionary love to Black folks in Africa and the Caribbean—places like Uganda, Haiti, and Jamaica—but will have nothing to do with extending that grace to Black folks in the United States. If, as a Black person, you immerse yourself in the history here and emerge with questions about how Blackness is constructed in the United States, these white folks will drop you as a lost cause and look for more docile Black folks. I recall a recent conversation on facebook with a former church friend from Bloomington, Indiana. This was during the Charlottesville white supremacist situation and I had posted something about the horrors of white supremacists. Former-church-friend who knew and loved me as a newly arrived "African" scolded me for calling members of that Charlottesville mob "supremacists." I countered with citing their chants about Jewish and Black people. Former-church-friend was upset with me for this and for posting "Black Lives Matter" stories on my time-line. Our mutual cancelation of each other was inevitable.

Again, this underscores the mark of Blackness that is ascribed to you when you critically push up against whiteness. As my situational Blackness moved from the outside realm of immigrant-African into the center of African American experience by learning about and empathizing with Black American history and culture, my relationship to Blackness be-came more nuanced and customized for this American space. I am still not "Black American," but I ask the questions, relate to and peel back the covers of American history, so that I have a sort of badge that marks my Blackness as a pan-African sort of Blackness. Now it is not only my heritage as West African and West Indian that grounds me comfortably across the Black world, in the motherland and the diaspora, it is also my attention to that proudly assertive part of the Black world that has been etched into the United States.

Historians and scholars have traced the creation of whiteness in the United States. After Frederick Douglass' master Mr. Auld stops his wife from teaching him how to read on the grounds that this skill will make him question his station as enslaved, Douglass realizes this as "a new and special revelation, dispelling a painful mystery, against which my youthful understanding had struggled, and struggled in vain to wit: the *white* man's power to perpetuate the enslavement of the Black man."[8] White overseers, poor and working-class, helped to terrorize enslaved human beings for their white employers. In his writings, Frederick Douglass narrates chilling stories about how far the overseer will go to enact the cruelty of the slave master. When an overseer violates a young Black woman and the master looks away, young "Freddy" is bewildered at the universality of cruelty exhibited by the two white men, both slave master and overseer. Looking back at this later, he reflects, "I think I now understand it. This treatment is a part of the system rather than a part of the man."[9] This revelation is buried deeply below the surface, forming the squirrely roots of American race and American history. Historian John Hope Franklin explains that the system was founded on

> regulatory statutes [which] were frankly repressive, and whites made no apologies for them. The laws represented the reduction to legal phraseology of the philosophy of the South with regard to the institution of slavery. Slaves had no standing in the courts: they could not be a party to a lawsuit; they could not offer testimony, except against another slave or a free Black; . . . a slave could not strike a white person, even in self-defense; but the killing of a slave, however malicious the act, was rarely regarded as murder. The rape of a female slave was regarded as a crime but only because it involved trespassing.[10]

It exposes a *system* that has constructed whiteness and Blackness, a system that has sprouted fruit and stems through reconstruction, Jim Crow, great migrations, gentrification, unequal access to education, healthcare, housing, and employment, and has brought us to our contemporary moment. When Frederick Douglass finally stands up against the cruel overseer in "The Last Flogging," he is also laying for us another root of resistance and insistence on the notions of equality, personhood, and liberation.[11] He is sending a message for the ages and for generations to come, that the flogging has to stop, that Black people matter.

When people say African Americans have been resilient in the face of all this, it is not an overstatement. Books, films, and music have been written and composed about this persistence and resilience. However, we have not spent much time thinking about the evolution of whiteness. What has become of that overseer and master? What became of that cold hatred that thought the ownership and use of other human beings was a God-given and ordained right? A study of the reconstruction era begins to peel back the layers that cover the evolution of that spirit. The KKK was founded and grew during the Reconstruction era. These are the same people who resisted desegregation when the Student Nonviolent Coordinating Committee (SNCC), Southern Christian Leadership Conference (SCLC), Congress of Racial Equality (Core), and the Black Panthers fought for racial justice in the 1950s and 1960s. In his autobiography, *Walking with the Wind*, John Lewis tells stories about the resistance the freedom riders faced when they attempted to help register Black voters or test the limits of desegregation at bus terminals, department stores, and restaurants. White folks would assemble to turn back American citizens who insisted on full freedoms. These white people would beat, kick, and spit at the patriots. They would extinguish their lit cigarettes on the necks of peaceful protesters. One vivid scene that I will always remember from *Walking with the Wind* is of a mob of white people of all ages apprehending a group of freedom riders. A gang of thugs catch hold of one of the riders, a peaceful white ally; call him a "nigger lover"; beat him senseless; and hold his head still for a child to scratch his face. I simply cannot get that vivid story out of my mind. And I wonder what became of the child. What does he remember of this episode? What attitudes were retained, and what did he or she pass on to his own children? That child might be about sixty-five years old today. That child may have children and grandchildren who walk our campuses, our board rooms, our high schools. Have we considered how folklore works and how stories are passed from one generation to another?

* * *

AM I RACIST?

In some cases the legacy of the social construction of whiteness lives on as an extreme, inhuman kind of apathy. It is all too easy to simply not care about people who fall outside of one's immediate circle of concern. White and black are opposites; as far away from one another as colors can get. Even when Blackness is not directly associated with negative ideas in the white American psyche, it is still at the very least perceived as dramatically "other." And when this otherness doesn't inspire the kind of passing curiosity Stephanie experienced as a recent African immigrant, or the active exclusion and mistreatment it has most often inspired against Black Americans, it can manifest as a simple but remarkably powerful absence of concern.

As a child and young adult I remember laughing—comfortably and genuinely—at jokes that disparaged or stereotyped people of other races. I wouldn't have ever told such jokes myself, and I would have objected to the telling of these jokes in the hearing of a person of that race. I wasn't, in other words, racist in the sense of holding opinions about racial hierarchy or harboring animosity toward people of other racial groups. I just didn't care enough about people who were sufficiently distant from me to allow such things to arouse my indignation. Just as the history of colonization could produce effects not only in social structures but also in the very minds and morals of those subject to it—such as the dynamic of the "comfortable" Black folks in the Nigerian golf club—so the history of racism in the United States has produced a desensitizing apathy among white folks, as my own childhood experience attests.

Stephanie's experiences and reflections on colonialism in Nigeria and Trinidad relate directly to the concept of institutional, systemic, implicit, or unconscious racism in the United States. Even decades after the colonizers had departed, the legacy of colonial influence remained. Similarly in American history, even decades after slavery was abolished with the 13th Amendment, the legacy of slavery remains. This illegal or extralegal American racism, like the shadow of European hegemony that hovered over Stephanie's Nigeria, is in many ways more difficult to recognize and confront than its more readily identifiable progenitor.

As with the concept of white privilege, it is impossible to argue against the existence of the phenomena that are referred to as systemic or implicit racism. On an individual psychological level, one of the clearest recent examples of the pervasive effects of implicit or unconscious racism occurred during the trial of Officer Mohamed Noor in Minnesota. Officer Noor mistakenly shot and killed a white woman in an alleyway while investigating the woman's own report of a person in distress in the area. One of the prosecutors in the trial asked Noor the following question during cross-examination: "Her whole blonde hair, pink T-shirt and all, that was all a threat to you?" The prosecutor's rhetorical point here is clear: most people implicitly or unconsciously associate the woman/pink T-shirt/blonde hair combination as nonthreatening. People like that generally wouldn't hurt a fly. It is, therefore, baffling that Officer Noor would react as if his life were in immediate danger.

The flip side of this is every example of police and citizen shootings of unarmed Black men in recent years: Trayvon Martin, Michael Brown, Philando Castille, Botham Jean, and so many others. These shootings are more understandable to white Americans and white jurors. Blonde white women in pink T-shirts don't look threatening to the average white American; Black men do. Part of this is what one might call implicit sexism; men are generally perceived as more dangerous than women. And the other part of it is what one might call implicit racism; Black Americans are generally perceived as more threatening than white Americans. Cases of Black women killed by the police also abound: Rekia Boyd, Brionna Taylor, Sandra Bland, Michelle Cusseaux, India Kager, and so many others. The combination of these characteristics also produces additional psychological or cultural associations: Black women face particular stereotypes that aren't shared either by white women or Black men, for example. The bottom line is this: when a white American sees a Black American, it is understandable to other white Americans that they would feel threatened, in danger, or at the very least uncomfortable.

This fact is enormously consequential and has very deep roots. The negative feeling described here is in some ways like garden-variety racism insofar as it involves a negative stereotype based on racial identity. And yet its psychological origin is not conscious malice. It is instead the result of a tragic combination of two things: (1) the multitude of pervasive effects stemming from the history of race-based slavery in the United States, and (2) the ordinary (and usually beneficial) human tendency to generalize.

There is no need to marshal the various statistical measurements of the disparities in economic well-being, the application of criminal justice, school suspension rates, educational opportunities, and health outcomes between white Americans and Black Americans to belabor the point or mislead my reader as to my intention. These disparities are significant and striking across almost every relevant variable, and are more significant and more striking across the board than the disparities between white Americans and any other minority racial or ethnic group in the United States. They are so pervasive and significant that even the most committed white supremacist would have a difficult time maintaining that they are the result of any real underlying disparity in individual ability or cultural attainment. Why do Black American mothers and their infants die at more than double the rate of their white counterparts in the United States?[12] Are white Americans just naturally two times healthier? Or could there be something else going on here?[13]

These real statistical disparities between white Americans and Black Americans, on average and across the United States, then interact with our ordinary human tendency to generalize. This generalizing tendency is usually an enormously helpful thing for human beings, and a crucial part of how we interact with other people and the world around us. At its most basic level, it's how we distinguish a human being from a fence post or a lion. Usually, things that look like fence posts don't have the linguistic capacity of human beings, so we don't waste our time talking to them. And things that look like lions often enough attempt to eat us, so we run. In these ways and innumerable, less obvious ones, our ability to generalize keeps us safe and helps us navigate the world effectively.

In the instance of race relations in the United States, most white Americans are the passive inheritors of this tragic combination of pervasive prejudice and generalization spanning generations. This cultural inheritance misleads many of us into automatically thinking that Black Americans are more like lions or fence posts than human beings. In its most overtly direct form, this manifests in the kind of ignorant, cruel verbal attack Tomiwa experienced while walking down the street soon after arriving in the United States. White Americans have been conditioned to either feel threatened and uncomfortable in the presence of Black Americans, or to simply ignore them.

In my own case growing up, it was the latter. The pervasive legacy of slavery was a big part of the reason why I barely ever encountered a Black person as a child. Almost no Black Americans live in the Napa Valley. According to recent statistics, the population of Napa is over 77 percent white and .76 percent Black.[14] Do Black Americans naturally tend to find vineyards ugly and wine disgusting? I find this unlikely.

Did my upbringing in a place where no Black Americans lived make me a racist? I did not suffer from any of the systemic disadvantages that regularly work to exclude Black Americans from ever living in a place like Napa. I didn't care at all about the people who did suffer from those systemic disadvantages. At the same time, I did not feel any animosity toward people of other races, and I didn't actively perpetuate negative stereotypes about them. I was young, and didn't have ready access to knowledge of African American history or personal acquaintance with Black Americans.

I lived on a white American island. I had a colorblindspot. Most importantly, I fell victim to the very ordinary human tendency to vastly underestimate the value of people who aren't familiar to us in some way. I didn't care because I didn't know better, but I also didn't know better because I didn't care. This dynamic is what enables and sustains the (mostly)

unconscious and unintentional phenomenon referred to as institutional
or systemic racism.

ARE AMERICAN INSTITUTIONS RACIST?

As a new professor at Northern Illinois University, I was in charge of
teaching a course called Democracy in America. This course was, for me,
something like what the Literature of the African Diaspora course was for
Stephanie in its impact on my developing thoughts about race and racism.
In this course we looked at American history through the conceptual lens
of liberty and equality. Teaching the unit on race in this course was what
initially led me to see the crucial importance of the African American
story not only to African Americans but to all Americans, and to the
American story as a whole.

In one of my first semesters teaching the course I had an astute Black
student who regularly brought up the concept of what she called "institutional racism." At the time, I didn't understand what she was referring
to. People can be racist, but what would it mean for an institution to be
racist?[15] Was it all institutions, or only some that were racist? Did the
institutions know that they were racist?

One day I simply asked her in class to explain what she meant by
the term. She said that institutional racism was when institutions were
designed by racists to perpetuate racial hierarchy. The Constitution was
an example of this. Though I treated her opinion seriously and respect-
fully in class and thanked her for her explanation, I remember thinking at
the time how implausible that sounded. To most white people today, the
concept of institutional racism sounds very much like a conspiracy theory.
Yes, some people in some institutions may be racist, but is it really possible
to bake racism into the very fabric of an institution so that it can have a
life of its own apart from the individuals within it?[16] If so, how can this be
done without even mentioning race or obvious hierarchical race relations
such as legal slavery?

One of my favorite trick questions when teaching the topic of slavery and the Constitution is to ask students how many times the word "slave" or "slavery" appears in the document before the 13th Amendment. I have often given students a quiz of initial Constitutional knowledge in which this question regularly appears. Before about 2014, much less than half of my students would get the correct answer (it's zero). Pointing this out was a way of getting students interested in delving deeper into the document and moving beyond their preconceptions of what it contained.

At some point, though, asking this question and explaining the answer began to have a very different effect in class. More and more of my white students already knew the answer and were eager to share it. I began to feel as if I were making a political point in asking the question, rather than stimulating curiosity among my students. White people had begun to react to renewed accusations of systemic racism in the wake of events such as the shooting of Trayvon Martin and the trial of George Zimmerman. Individual Americans might be racist, but America herself was not. Sure, my white students would say, slavery existed, but did you know that it isn't mentioned even once in the Constitution until it was abolished in the 13th Amendment?

My Black student was right about the existence of the various phenomena associated with institutional racism, but her explanation about racist institution designers can be misleading. There is more than one way to be racist, and they aren't all created equal. Racism exists on a spectrum stretching from conscious, active hatred of people of another race all the way to unconscious, unintentional ignoring of people of another race. On the one end of the spectrum is vice; on the other end is lack of virtue.

Something similar might be said with respect to other vices, like cowardice. Cowardice can range from failing to stand up for a friend because you are afraid of being disliked by others to failing to jump into a bear enclosure at the zoo to save a stranger from being mauled. They are both failings of courage. But are they both cowardice? Is the bystander who doesn't risk life and limb in the uncertain hope of saving a complete stranger the same as the person who doesn't risk social disapprobation to stand up for a close friend? Most of us would want to distinguish between the two, and would likely hesitate to call the bystander at the zoo a coward. Actual cowardice requires a combination of a few things: (1) an accurate knowledge of a negative or threatening situation; (2) a clear ability to act positively and constructively in this situation; and (3) a failure to do so. In the case of the zoo bystander, it isn't clear that jumping into the bear enclosure will be a positive and constructive response to the situation; they might just both get mauled.

The case of racism seems similar. Everything on the racism spectrum is a failing of racism's opposite, which I would call charity. In that way it's all the same thing. But in another way, it would probably make sense to distinguish between the two ends of the racism spectrum the same way we would in the case of cowardice. The conscious, active hatred of people of another race is the paradigm or pinnacle case of racism. The consciously endorsed opinion of racial hierarchy, such as the one that animated European colonization of Africa and that Stephanie relates being affected by as a child and young adult, follows closely on its heels. Racism, like cowardice, requires the combination of a few ingredients: (1) the availability of knowledge regarding the humanity of people of other races; (2) opportunities for treating people of other races in ways opposed to this knowledge; and (3) actually acting in these ways (including speaking as an action).

But what about where I was? I was ignorant and apathetic, but not unusually or willfully so. I unconsciously and unintentionally ignored people of other races, people who didn't look like me. My colorblindspot meant that I lived on a white island and was content to mostly remain there. At the same time, though, I didn't treat people of other races in an in- or subhuman way. I was at least a step or two away from the British colonizers of the eighteenth and nineteenth centuries. And what about where American institutions are? How many of them have been created by conscious racists to actively perpetuate racial hierarchy? Or how many of them have reflected and sustained an assumed racial superiority, explicitly or implicitly?

Institutional racism in the United States reflects some elements of the European colonization of African peoples, and some elements of European colonization of Caribbean, Central, and South American peoples, but it is also unique in important ways. These unique elements are what led Stephanie to experience racial identity in a different way upon her arrival in the United States than she had in postcolonial Nigeria. Institutional racism in the United States has usually arisen when institutional designers have had the same kinds of colorblindspots I had (and to some extent certainly still have)—not conscious endorsement of racial hierarchy or active animosity toward people of other races, but a kind of passive or partially willful ignorance and apathy. The results of the designs of such people are institutions that both (1) reflect and reinforce existing legal, cultural, and economic racial hierarchies, and (2) enable and sometimes sanction the kind of personal racism that is the paradigm case we tend to associate with the term.[17]

Defined in this way, the most obvious case of institutional racism in the United States is the Constitution. But here I think the term "institutional racism" begins to betray its own cause. The most conservative defender of the Constitution wouldn't be able to plausibly deny the truth of the two points above when applied to it. By remaining strictly neutral with respect to the institution of slavery while strengthening the political society within which slavery existed, the Constitution both (1) necessarily reinforced existing racial hierarchies in the law, the economy, and society and (2) enabled the flourishing of personal racism by better securing the lives, liberties, and property rights of the almost-entirely-white freemen and slaveholders against potential resistance on the part of racism's victims.

But do these things make the Constitution a racist document? Does it make all of the Constitution's Framers—people like Alexander Hamilton, James Wilson, or Gouverneur Morris—racist themselves for their role in contributing to it? If so, how could Frederick Douglass plausibly call the Constitution a "glorious liberty document?"[18] How could Abraham Lincoln claim that the Constitution's Framers put the institution of slavery "in the course of ultimate extinction?"[19] Were these ridiculously far-fetched or completely disingenuous arguments?

I think that they aren't far-fetched or deceitful and, therefore, that something is going wrong when we apply the same term of "racist" to both

the exploitative white supremacist slaveholder and to the political document (as well as its authors) that first ignored racism and then was used
as the groundwork for working against it. Labeling someone a "coward"
for deciding against jumping into the bear pit in a risky attempt to rescue
a stranger is unlikely to affect that person's behavior in the future. He will
more likely dismiss the label as obviously inapplicable.

A similar point holds for the labeling of the Constitution or its authors
collectively as "racist." As I've defined "institutional racism" above, the
label clearly applies. The connection of the Constitution and its authors
to the spectrum of racism is clear. But the Constitution and its authors, in
their writing of it, are sufficiently far from the clearest cases of racism to
make the reaction of dismissal or denial the most likely one on the part of
those who identify with it. They appear more like the zoo bystander than
the silent friend. And by failing to discriminate between distant points on
the racism spectrum, those who charge the Constitution and its authors
with racism are in fact unnecessarily discrediting the argument they are
trying to make.

The truths in their arguments are important and require clear recognition: the fact that the Constitution doesn't directly or explicitly contravene
slavery is not only a troubling omission but a real moral and practical
failure of the document. It is a failure of its authors, some of whom were
personally opposed to slavery. It led to the actual collapse of the United
States in the Civil War. This was a failure not only of charity but of justice with respect to human beings who were conceived to belong to another race. In these ways it is similar to garden-variety or paradigmatic
racism. But it is also very different from ordinary racism. For one thing,
the Constitution itself is a written document, not a person. It can't perform racist actions with racist feelings the way a human being can—it
can't even tie its own shoe. And though its authors were human beings,
the Constitution doesn't have a single author; it was signed by thirty-
nine people, and many more contributed in some way to its construction.
Some of these people had wildly different opinions about slavery and fell
on nearly opposite ends of the racism spectrum—ranging from the viru-
lently antislavery Gouverneur Morris of Pennsylvania to the determinedly

proslavery Charles Pinckney of South Carolina. About the only thing all of these people agreed on was the need for political union on the basis of the principles of the Revolution. If the Constitution has any single purpose, this is it.

The Constitution's authors as a group didn't set out to perpetuate or protect slavery, just as the Constitution doesn't do what Justice Taney said it does in the *Dred Scott* decision—"distinctly and expressly" affirm the rights of slaveholders. This wasn't the Constitution's and its authors' problem. Their problem was the same as my problem growing up in wine country: most of them didn't really care either way. Those who were antislavery didn't care enough to move the group as a whole away from the "care not" policy made famous by Stephen Douglas in his debates with Lincoln nearly a century later. Just as Douglas claimed to "care not whether slavery be voted up or down," so the Constitution's authors ultimately took a neutral policy toward slavery in order to achieve political union. This allowed slavery to continue and flourish under the protection of the Constitutional Union. In calling this situation by the very same name used to describe personal, intentional acts of injustice motivated by opinions and feelings of racial superiority, though, those who call the Constitution and its authors "racist" give their opponents a too-easy excuse to dodge the real argument. The real argument is that the Constitution didn't directly or explicitly lay the groundwork for the abolition of slavery, and that it indirectly supported the freedom of states and individuals to perpetuate the horrific act of enslavement and to give free rein to their racist attitudes. The Constitution's relationship to slavery is different from the slaveholder's relationship to slavery; calling both of them by the same name only weakens the point that critics of the Constitution are trying to make.

As in the case of "white privilege," "institutional racism" is a term that refers to something that clearly exists. In either case, the presence of the relevant phenomena (as a scientist might say) is difficult to deny. But, as in the case of "white privilege," I wonder whether "institutional racism" is unhelpful and misleading. Like "white privilege," "institutional racism" tends to have one of two effects on the average white American: (1)

defensive denial; or (2) passive, self-congratulatory guilt. The first is a typical sight at white American family gatherings, and the second is seen in most university classrooms. Both are unhelpful. Neither leads to productive conversations about the righting of wrongs or the pursuit of justice; neither, in fact, leads to genuine conversations at all.

Knowledge and Ignorance

A BLACK FAMILY IN WHITE AMERICA

When my children were young, I would go to the local Bloomington library to find movies and books that they might enjoy. We quickly got through the Disney movies: *Little Mermaid, Cinderella, Pocahontas*, and *Lion King*. All these were wonderful offerings. My two Black daughters and one Black son loved these films. But as a mother, with memories of a white doll named Ingrid, I yearned for another set of cinematic experiences that showed them something of themselves. I wanted them to know that kids who looked like them were also worthy of attention. *Lion King* had been the closest thing to a focus on the motherland, but there are actually no African people in it. There are no people in it at all. And, to boot, the animal voices are mostly British and American actors. This was no help. Then in 2005, when my kids were four, five, and seven, *Madagascar* came out and I thought Disney might finally remember that there are Black kids in the world who want to see themselves on screen. The excitement in the Shonekan household was high. Off we went to the theater, not knowing much about the film except that it was set in Africa. My heart dropped as we watched and saw that, once again, Disney's treatment of Africa was not about the people, but about the animals. It sends a certain kind of message when a major media company chooses to overlook the people of an entire continent and its diaspora, not once, but two times. (Counting all

Race and the American Story. Stephanie Shonekan and Adam Seagrave, Oxford University Press.
© Oxford University Press 2024. DOI: 10.1093/oso/9780197767689.003.0004

the sequels of both *Lion King* and *Madagascar* only amplifies the futility of this situation.)[1]

The same frustrations simmered in me as a mother as the children became avid readers. They loved book series like *Junie B. Jones*, *Percy Jackson*, *The Hunger Games*, *Gregor the Overlander*, and *Divergent*. Here again there was a dearth of choices for my children. What happens when you watch movies and read books with characters and heroes that do not look or live like you? My oldest daughter is our most avid reader. As a young teenager, she would devour fiction—any book she could get her hands on. We would go to Barnes and Noble, or Borders or the local library, and we would browse the young adult section. Book covers promised stories of adventure and romance with protagonists who were pale-skinned and blond haired. Once in a while, a book would appear with Black characters, but they were always stories about the civil rights movement, or violence, or resilience. It was never just a fun, fantasy world. One day after we searched for some options, she turned to me and asked, "Mom, why don't they write ordinary books about us?" This struck me deeply because I know the damage I received when my teenage mind was filled with the unattainable aesthetics and qualities of whiteness. But we had made the choice to leave our predominantly Black country and move to a predominantly white country. We would have to learn to deal with this.

When I got my first faculty job at Columbia College Chicago, friends advised me vigorously against buying a house in Naperville. They could not understand why I, a reasonably progressive African woman, would consider taking my family to live in a predominantly conservative, republican, white suburb. After all, they urged, there are alternatives that better suit an African family. Hyde Park, Evanston, Bronzeville, and Oak Park were mentioned as places where we would "fit in." I suppose the logic was that we would be better off living in an area where there are more people who look like us. As a Black studies scholar who has lived in the United States for many years, I was not naive about race in America. My husband and I appreciated our friends' advice. We joked that if we had been scared of white folks, we would not have moved to the United States. But our more serious response was that the excellent public schools there should not be out of our reach because we are Black. Naperville would just have to deal with five additional Black people.

We never really regretted our move to Naperville. We found great neighbors and formed lifelong friendships with people who I might never have gotten to know in my other walks of life. I learned that their politics ranged from far left to far right; and that many of them knew little about the world beyond the borders of Illinois. But perhaps the greatest lesson came from the reflections on race that had been inspired by the very acute experience of being a minority in a privileged white neighborhood.

The life of a minority is full of oppressive potholes, which "majority folks" never have to think of. We constantly pull out our imaginary race lenses to study each daily encounter in this white world, to see if there is more than meets the eye, to see if our perceptions of race and racism are ever legitimate. Living in a predominantly white neighborhood, this impulse is magnified. I had lots of conversations with white friends who cited the touted label of a "postracial America" and the incredible fact that, at that time, the US president was a Black man.[2] I understood that they believed in their heart of hearts that the realities of legalized racism were in the distant past. My response to them was always this: You cannot assume to know for sure if racism exists if you are not a racial minority yourself.

After several of these frustrating discussions, I've had to come up with an analogy to explain my position: I'm a woman who enjoys watching sports like soccer and basketball. When grown men fall to the ground and roll around because they've been accidentally kicked in the groin, I would love to shout at them to suck it up and keep playing. But I've been told by all the men in my life that this occurrence is horribly painful. I will never know what being kicked in the groin feels like because I'm not a man. In the same way, a nonminority will never really know what being a minority feels like or what the perceptions of race are from this end of the color spectrum. When I offer this analogy, I usually see brief sparks of enlightenment in my friends' eyes, which is encouraging. What is left to be seen is whether these sparks catch the fire of enlightenment or fizzle away into the smoky abyss of ignorance. Almost daily, there are new encounters that present opportunities for complicated reflections on race. Consider these examples:

On a rare occasion when I could not attend my monthly book club meeting, my white lady friends argued about the selection of a new book for the following month. Someone proposed the book *The Help* about Black maids in the South who worked for white women during the civil rights movement. One of the book club ladies, my closest friend among them, objected to this suggestion feeling that it would be unfair to select that book because I, the only Black member of the club, might feel uncomfortable reading and discussing this book. The other ladies insisted that I would be fine with this book because after all, this book was not about Blacks like me. They reasoned that I am African, not African American, so I should have the necessary distance to simply enjoy the book as good fiction.

In a sense, it was good to know that our five-year involvement in the book club and their association with me had sensitized these women to the fact that Black folks are not a homogeneous clump of humanity. It's good that they had reached a stage where they could afford me the privilege of a nuanced Black identity. But there is an irony here. In rushing to appear racially astute, they lost sight of the obvious. That even though I am "African," in this country I am still "Black." This is America, where skin color is still the immediate signifier of race, a fact that prevents a collective intellectual shift toward a more thoughtful consideration of ethnicity and subcultural significance. In short, to most Americans who don't know me, I am not West African, or Nigerian, or West Indian, or Trinidadian. I am simply Black.

A book club discussion of *The Help* would likely focus on the hierarchical power structure of the historical white–Black relationship, therefore invoking in me responses from my Black identity, not my African identity. My book club friends meant well, but race in white suburban America is so much more complex for the minority than it is for the dominant group. Over the preceding five years, in all my imparting of cultural awareness, I had not succeeded in conveying the true and deep essence of what it means to be Black. Their "colorblindspot" remained, at least to some extent. If I am the primary source for trying to educate them out of this blindness, there is a dearth of supplemental resources for them in the media.

For my children, the Naperville experience was also interesting. They thrived in school and had wonderful friends. They were too young to be burdened with these disturbing realities, I told myself. So I silently cringed when I saw their white friends constantly touching their hair in a mixture of wonder and confusion. I reminded myself that these kids were just responding naturally to something new, i.e., a Black person in close proximity. But other episodes were not so harmless. When my eleven-year-old daughter and her best friend (who is biracial) were not cast in a speaking or singing role for the school play after working very hard to prepare for the auditions, I overheard them lamenting that it was probably because they were Black. Sadly, when I attended the play, I saw that indeed no Black student had been given a speaking or solo singing role. Perhaps all the white kids were indeed better than the Black kids who auditioned, but that does not prevent the perceptions from taking root, nor the unfortunate conclusions from sprouting. I heard from other Black parents that this is the norm, so most of the few Black kids stopped auditioning. However, banished to the anonymous ranks of the ensemble, my daughter and her friend decided that they would be the best chorus members in that play. They produced the biggest smiles on the stage that night.

But in the case of the children too, it's not just about being Black. The few African Americans in their school, most of whom navigated their world as a tight group, seemed to shun my kids because they did not quite fit the profile. They spoke "too proper," wore their hair too natural, and had too many white friends. So my children had to find their own path somewhere in the middle—certainly not white, yet not completely "Black." As parents, we had always resisted handing our children those imaginary race lenses I mentioned earlier, but each of them, individually, seems to be finding their own way to those lenses.

The question remains: Should we have hearkened to the voices of reason and stayed away from Naperville? Living there made us acutely aware of our identity and our perceptions of race in America. Because we were so clearly "the other" there, we had to work hard to elevate our sense of self in order to proudly come to terms with who we were as Africans and as Black folks. Plus we learned more about white folks than we would have if we had lived in a predominantly Black neighborhood. Naperville is still certainly a distinct suburb with its own unique character, but is it really different from most white suburbs, or for that matter most social and professional spaces in the United States? If anything, living in Naperville prepared us to live, work, and interact with mainstream America where perceptions of discrimination and realities of racism are still interwoven into the fabric of daily existence.

MAKE AMERICA GREAT AGAIN

This slogan, "Make America Great Again," is a great example of how important it is to consider perspectives. If you were a middle-class white Anglo-Saxon family growing up in the suburbs of mid-America in the 1950s, seeing the fruits of your labor in that Ford assembly plant, watching *Gunsmoke* and going to sock hops, making and eating apple pie, going undisturbed to restaurants and department stores, then this slogan makes sense to you. With the state of the economy, the plunging GDP, the export of factories to Asia and Central and South America as companies chase their optimal capitalist dreams, the prevalence of trashy reality television shows, and an evolved contemporary form of the music you loved, your quality of life is not the same as your grandparents'. I get it. But if you are thinking more widely about the various groups of Americans, and if you zoom in on the profile of African Americans in the 1950s or really, at any other time in American history, it is difficult to find the greatness, except, perhaps, in the music.[3] A Jim Crow America created a tough life for African Americans with limited trajectories of what was truly achievable. The potential for "great" employment, education, and social access was stemmed by apartheid-like policies corralling their movements and ability for unrestricted upward mobility.

If we zoom in further to that slice of time that has often been cited for the verity of this slogan—Make America Great Again—we can find evidence for the ungreatness of America for African Americans. Indeed, this was the era of "racial terrorism," to borrow a term from Equal Justice Initiative founder and executive director and writer of *Just Mercy* Bryan Stevenson. One needs only to explore names of people like Emmett Till who are listed on the EJI website to understand the tense, uncomfortable, and unjust world that African Americans were living in during the 1950s. If we cast our lens back before and after the 1950s, we will not find an era that was "great" for the majority of African Americans. A "Make America Great" slogan would probably have wide support, but the addition of the word "again" at the end of that slogan is inaccurate for all Americans— perhaps accurate for some, but not for all.

Often Oprah and Obama are cited as examples of African Americans who have achieved great heights. This citation is often followed by the question: "so why can't all African Americans reach these heights?" The question sounds harmless, but it is disingenuous at best. If we examine the systemic extensions of the last four hundred years, it is reasonable to state that the glass ceiling, though cracked for some, is still sturdy and durable. Without going into the employment and incarceration numbers, which are available on a quick google search, we can stay hovering on the surface of perception and reception: Black men are still feared for their beautiful physicality. Depending on who is beholding their dark skins and very presence, they may "look like a demon," which is what officer Darren Wilson testified after shooting unarmed Mike Brown,[4] or they may be seen as "a super double caffeine dream" as Indie Arie sings in her "Chocolate High" duet with Musiq Soulchild (2009). Black women have historically been dismissed or disdained, accused of occupying the "angry Black woman" trope or the oversexualized Black female trope.

When I think about the traumatic implications of these perceptions, I also turn inward, to the result of these perceptions on Black folks. When we turn inward, we are confronted with additional layers of perceptions that make our daily lives and existences cloudy, unclear, unhealthy. The psychological unraveling at every turn is a quotidian reality. Take a recent example: Our college-age son lives in an apartment in Sunderland, Massachusetts, with his two white teammates. They are close friends, trust each other, and live well together. The apartment complex is large, with many units. This is Sunderland, so there aren't too many Black folks there, nor indeed in the entire region of "the valley." All was well. Then one morning our son calls, a little distressed. Apparently, when he woke up to go on a run that morning, he noticed that the back window of his car was smashed. There had been a storm the night before and he assumed that some debris had hit the car. As soon as we heard this, we immediately wondered if this was a hate crime. Understand our thought process: his car was parked between two other cars. It was not at the end of the parking lot. No other cars in that parking lot were damaged. How could this have happened so randomly? And at the same time, it totally could have been random. But as Black parents of a Black son who is over six feet tall, we have to wonder if he is observed as a demon in that apartment complex. If this had happened to his roommates, their parents would never have to consider this as a possibility. That is the reason why the country is not yet "great." There have been strides toward justice, but the erosive impact of even the last seventy years is still heavy on the national psyche, whichever way we look at it.

* * *

IGNORE-ANCE

My own college experiences were similar to those of the white residents of Sunderland, Massachusetts. Between the two undergraduate institutions I attended after high school—the US Naval Academy at Annapolis and Thomas Aquinas College in California—I encountered precisely two Black students. Because these schools are both relatively cut off from the outside world and located in overwhelmingly white areas, these were also the only Black people I encountered during this five-year period. One of my roommates at the Naval Academy whom I remember very fondly was

Black. I remember his last name was White. There was one Black student at Thomas Aquinas College in a student body of about 350. We had different circles of friends.

Relating my experiences as a young adult at these institutions to Stephanie's description of her white lady friends in the book club is both illuminating and embarrassing. I was, admittedly, very young; but at that time I hadn't even achieved the level of awareness attained by the book club members who thought Stephanie wouldn't be affected by reading *The Help*. The Black student at Thomas Aquinas College was an African immigrant; the Black student at the Naval Academy was African American. I didn't mentally distinguish between the two in this way at all. They were both simply "Black" to me. I hadn't known or cared enough to think about this difference. Nor, of course, had I taken the next step of realizing that our artificially racially dichotomous culture in the United States caused most white people like me to see both of them in these simple colorized terms—and that this social perception in turn affected their own self-conscious identities and experiences in significant ways.

I was unaware of all of this, but this ignorance did not influence my college choices directly. I didn't target these colleges because they were almost devoid of Black students. Whether because of my own particular interests and personality, or because of the white world and culture in which I grew up, I just happened to be attracted to two types of institutions of higher education that either don't appeal to or aren't accessible to many Black Americans. Whatever the reason, I was able (without my own awareness or intention) to extend my ignorance of anything related to the African American experience and its history by another four years.

We can't care about something we don't know about. More importantly, though, we also don't care about everything we do know about. Our field of ignorance is large and problematic. Our field of "ignore"-ance is also large and even more problematic. Over one thousand people around the world are murdered every day.[5] Over eight thousand children around the world die from hunger every day.[6] Most people don't know these numbers off hand, but everyone knows that large numbers of people are murdered every day, that large numbers of children starve every day, that terrible injustices are being committed somewhere in the world every minute of every day. And, usually for morally acceptable reasons related to our ability or capacity, we simply ignore these things. Martin Luther King Jr.'s statement that "injustice anywhere is a threat to justice everywhere" tends to go in one ear and out the other.

Our ignore-ance of global injustices is understandable and, most ethicists would argue, morally acceptable, at least in many cases. The case of pervasive injustices occurring within our own political society is very different. Ignorance in this case is inexcusable, and ignore-ance is morally problematic. Nearly everyone in the United States knew about the institution of slavery from the seventeenth century through the eve of the Civil War. Most white Americans ignored it. Nearly everyone in the United States has known about segregation, racial discrimination, and persistent racial inequalities from the time of the Civil War to today. Most white Americans, including myself for most of my life, have ignored it. Why disturb the comfortable affluence of a Naperville or a Napa by worrying about persistent racism and its ubiquitous effects?

My own ignore-ance continued as well through graduate school at Notre Dame, where I studied the American Founding and came to focus on the concepts of natural law and natural rights. At Notre Dame, as at Thomas Aquinas College and the US Naval Academy, I did not encounter Black people and continued to ignore issues of racial injustice in the United States. My ignorance of American politics and history was increasingly being driven out by knowledge, but my ignore-ance of African Americans was not yet being filled up by charity.

A stint as a visiting professor at Pepperdine University immediately following graduate school did not—needless to say!—change this trend. Pepperdine is itself much more diverse than its surroundings in Malibu, with 6.82 percent of its students identifying as Black or African American.[7] Malibu, much like Napa, is 92.7 percent white and 1.1 percent Black.[8] Of course, it could be that just as Black Americans don't like vineyards and wine, they also don't like mansions on hillsides overlooking the ocean!

It wasn't until a few years later, as I was teaching my Democracy in America course at Northern Illinois University, that I began to wake up

to the urgent importance of issues of racial injustice both in themselves
and to the American story. I had always been a big fan of the American
Revolution; of that exciting time when American principles of liberty and
equality were at their purest, inspiring passion sufficient to motivate a war
for independence against the most powerful nation in the world.[9] Much of
the course involved tracing the echoes of this revolutionary passion across
American history.

As I was doing so, I frequently tripped on examples of African
Americans arguing that American Revolutionary arguments applied to
their own circumstances of unjust enslavement—and with even greater
intensity and urgency than they did to the circumstances of the Anglo-
European colonists. The American Revolutionaries had abandoned the
conventional ground of "British rights" for the expansive ground of "natural rights": the rights that inalienably attach to all human beings by virtue
of their very existence and essence. Once white Americans shifted to this
ground, they necessarily—if mostly unintentionally—placed the basis of
their rights within equal reach of African Americans. The "slavery" under
which white American revolutionaries suffered violated their natural
rights in a remote, logical way; the slavery under which African Americans
suffered violated their natural rights in a direct, egregious, tangible way.
The arguments of African American advocates for abolition and justice
on American Revolutionary principles were persuasive, even compelling.

There was Prince Hall petitioning the Massachusetts legislature in 1777
to abolish slavery, and expressing his "astonishment, that it has never
been considered, that every principle from which America has acted in
the course of her unhappy difficulties with Great-Britain, pleads stronger
than a thousand arguments in favor of your Petitioners."[10] There was
Phillis Wheatley eloquently pointing out "the strange Absurdity of their
Conduct whose Words and Actions are so diametrically opposite. How
well the Cry for Liberty, and the reverse Disposition for the exercise of
oppressive Power over others agree, I humbly think it does not require the
Penetration of a Philosopher to Determine."[11]

There was Frederick Douglass, excoriating Christian white America
for its ignore-ance of the institution of slavery while commemorating the

4th of July: "The existence of slavery in this country brands your republicanism as a sham, your humanity as a base pretence, and your Christianity
as a lie." Douglass's words here are worth noting carefully, especially by
white Americans today. He didn't say merely that slaveholders can't be
genuine (small-r) republicans, decent human beings, or true Christians.
He also didn't say that the perpetuation of slavery represented a problem
for the future of republicanism, or that American Christians everywhere
should work toward abolition. His phrasing was stark, and his words left no
wiggle room whatsoever. In Douglass's view, the institution of slavery and
the conglomeration of American Revolutionary principles–humanity–
Christianity were like two solids trying to occupy the same space—if the
one is there, the other can't be.[12]

There was W. E. B. Du Bois in his 1905 Niagara Movement speech
just before the founding of the NAACP, arguing in the following stirring
language: "The battle we wage is not for ourselves alone but for all true
Americans. It is a fight for ideals, lest this, our common fatherland, false
to its founding, become in truth the land of the thief and the home of
the Slave—a by-word and a hissing among the nations for its sounding
pretensions and pitiful accomplishment." Du Bois, just like Frederick
Douglass, Prince Hall, Phillis Wheatley, and many others, argued that
"all true Americans" are intimately concerned with the struggle of Black
Americans for equal civil rights and basic justice. If the United States is
supposed to be based on more than the sheer power of the stronger, and
to trace its beginnings not to "accident and force" but to "reflection and
choice," Du Bois's battle for racial equality and justice has to be the battle
of all true Americans.[13]

I was (and am) persuaded by these arguments. Any one of them is compelling, taken alone, and taken all together they are like an irresistible av-
alanche of reasonability. Irresistible, that is, by everything except the other
Douglas's indomitable "I care not."

Even this last bastion of ignore-ance, though, is ultimately overcome
by an argument Abraham Lincoln made in an unpublished note about the
implications of slavery:

If A can prove, however conclusively, that he may, of right, enslave
B. Why may not B snatch the same argument, and prove equally, that
he may enslave A?

You say A is white, and B is Black. It is *color*, then; the lighter,
having the right to enslave the darker? Take care. By this rule, you are
to be slave to the first man you meet, with a fairer skin than your own.

You do not mean *color* exactly? You mean the whites are *intellectually* the superiors of the Blacks, and, therefore have the right to
enslave them? Take care again. By this rule, you are to be slave to the
first man you meet, with an intellect superior to your own.

But, say you, it is a question of *interest*; and, if you can make it
your *interest*, you have the right to enslave another. Very well. And if
he can make it his interest, he has the right to enslave you.[14]

Lincoln's stream-of-consciousness debate with himself here breaks
down the absurdity of arguments for race-based slavery in the kind of
commonsensical-yet-profound way only Lincoln could. It does so, moreover, while appealing to the most reliable psychological force known to
humanity: self-interest. It was self-interest that had originated and continued the institution of slavery; it was self-interest that led Jefferson to
defend the slaveholding interest at the time of the Missouri Crisis; it was
self-interest that motivated the vehement defenses of slavery that emerged
in the second quarter of the eighteenth century; and it was self-interest
that motivated Lincoln to see the evil of slavery clearly and to oppose its
extension.[15]

By his own account, Lincoln had always hated slavery. He didn't care
about it though—it was a "minor question" for him—until the Kansas-
Nebraska Act in 1854 raised the prospect of slavery's extension beyond the
Southern states.[16][36] This brought the issue of slavery to Lincoln's front
door for the first time, and got him thinking along the self-interested
lines he described in his notes.[17] Slavery in Georgia or South Carolina
was undoubtedly a bad thing; it just wasn't an urgent problem for white
politicians in the North like Lincoln. There were more pressing political matters to attend to, like the war with Mexico, the annexation of

Texas, and the Manifest Destiny of westward expansion. As long as the evils of slavery remained a peculiarity of Southern states, never explicitly endorsed by the federal government, people like Lincoln could rest satisfied that slavery was "in the course of ultimate extinction."[18] Lincoln was like Jefferson, Madison, Hamilton, Washington, and numerous other well-meaning architects of the American political system; he wanted slavery to end eventually, just on his own comfortable timeline and with minimal cost to those like himself who were already enjoying the benefits of the exceptional American system.

Lincoln's reasoning, combined with the political developments of the 1850s that threatened the extension of slavery, led him to a moment of identification with enslaved African Americans. If it was mere power and interest, not right or Divine Providence, that matched "white" with "free" and "Black" with "slave," the situation of enslaved people in the United States might one day be Lincoln's own. Lincoln hated slavery but ignored it when it only affected other people; he hated it *and* cared about opposing it when he could imagine it affecting him. Empathy grew out of self-interest.

TEACHING AND LEARNING

The case of Lincoln highlights a truth of absolutely crucial importance for achieving genuine social justice while improving race relations in the United States today. It is one thing to know about injustice; it is quite another to care about rectifying injustice. The one does not necessarily—and, sadly, does not even usually—follow the other. There are three ways of building this connection, given the parameters of human nature: (1) proximity to the injustice, which makes ignoring it more uncomfortable; (2) religion, which can inspire direct empathy and identification with the other; and (3) self-interest, which can lead to a facsimile of empathy and identification and is sometimes good enough from a practical social perspective. Proximity is an effective route but can be avoided or excused by social segregation or simply turning a blind eye; the religion route was taken by many abolitionist leaders and continues to be influential for some religious leaders today; Lincoln seems to have gone the self-interest route.

My own journey to caring was perhaps unusual. There was no catalyzing event or transformative moment. It didn't happen by getting to know people who are Black and relating to them on a personal level. I didn't look on the horizon and see injustice coming for me if I didn't start caring about others. For me, it was the combination of pursuing truth and living the Christian faith. I cared deeply about both, and I realized that Frederick Douglass was right: I couldn't care about truth and Christian charity without caring about the historic, continuing, and systemic injustices being perpetrated by one group of Americans against another under my very nose.[19]

And yet there is a deep question today about the ability of Christian churches and their leaders to stand for justice. The vigor with which many evangelical Christians supported Trump's "Make America Great Again" campaign was confusing to many Americans, particularly those who were convinced that America had never actually been great for people defined as nonwhite and treated unjustly on that basis. The reluctance and resistance shown by many Christian churches and pastors to address racial injustices has been palpable in the last few years. People like Stephanie's former-church-friend, who spend all of their charity on Africans while disdaining African Americans, or who are willing to put a BLM sign in their yard but wouldn't be caught in public with someone outside their tax bracket or zip code, still abound in American society. Nor is this only a recent phenomenon. In his "What to the Slave Is the Fourth of July?" speech, Frederick Douglass excoriated the Christian churches for their failures to oppose slavery. Martin Luther King Jr.'s "Letter from a Birmingham Jail" is devoted explicitly to similar failures on the part of the Christian clergymen who had written to him disapprovingly. Just as some Christian churches and clergymen twisted the Bible message into an expression of support for slavery prior to the Civil War, some Christian churches and clergymen today continue to downplay or ignore ongoing issues of racism and its effects in American society.

Christians such as these betray the true Christian message. True Christian conviction is built on truth and love, which must be systematically ignored or violently twisted to avoid vehemently opposing racism at every turn. In my own case, Christian conviction led me to begin teaching a course on African American political thought at Northern Illinois University. I wanted to help lead others out of ignorance about African American history and the crucial contributions of Black Americans to the American story. Most white students knew nothing about this, and many Black students didn't see clearly how their story fit in to the American story. My hope was that my course would help in constructing a broader and better "We" by showing both white and Black students how their more particular "we's" had contributed to common goals and fought for common causes throughout American history.

I wasn't always completely successful, of course. It is true that many students, both white and Black, seemed to be affected in exactly the way I had hoped. I was opening up a whole new world to my white students, and I was showing my nonwhite students that their story might not be simply opposed to the white American story. But I still had a long way to go in adjusting my own lens to see the topics I was teaching more broadly and, as a result, more accurately.

The first example of this learning experience came when I was teaching at Northern Illinois University. One day after class I was approached by one of my best students, a Black woman, who expressed her concern that I was dwelling in a too-sympathetic way on Jefferson's self-understanding of his situation as a slaveholder. In hindsight this criticism made sense to me; I initially tended to identify more with Jefferson's thought processes than with the perspectives of the people he held as slaves. It was instinctively more interesting to me to analyze the minds of slaveholders—even if I strongly disagreed with their practice of enslavement—than it was to analyze the minds of enslaved people. I had initially seen the slaveholders like Jefferson as more like me, and it is all too human to be more interested in people one perceives as like themselves than in people one perceives to be different. Now, there's nothing wrong with being interested in Thomas

Jefferson—but there is something much righter with being equally interested in the people he held in slavery.

This was the first time I was really forced to confront what people today might call my own "implicit bias"—my unconscious tendency to sympathize with and privilege the part of humanity that is more familiar to me over the part that is new or different. I am forever grateful to this student for making me aware of this tendency, and introducing me to the uncomfortable, painful, incessant, and extremely beneficial practice of forcing myself out of it. Since this time, I have constantly striven to teach Jefferson, Lincoln, and other white Americans in a more nuanced way. I have tried to teach about these figures not only as potential objects of understanding and praise but also as potential objects of moral disapprobation, pity, and even condemnation—in other words, not as white people like me but as humans like all of us. Unconscious bias is easy and automatic. It is human. Viewing people of different backgrounds and ancestries as fellow humans is, strangely, not so easy. It takes constant work, and often an initial push such as the one this student gave me after class.

Another moment of learning while teaching occurred at my next stop, the University of Missouri. I was again approached after my African American political thought class, this time by two female students, and confronted with the criticism that my syllabus didn't include any female authors. This may be as difficult for my readers to believe as it is for me to believe in hindsight myself: I taught an entire semester-long course on African American political thought that didn't include a single female author on the syllabus. I can almost hear Stephanie and my other female Race and the American Story colleagues chuckling disbelievingly to themselves at this. I immediately recognized this moment as similar to the Jefferson sympathizer moment some years before—of course I had automatically gravitated toward the male authors with whom I was familiar, and of course this was not the most thoroughly illuminating approach to the topics I was covering. Because of these students and the female colleagues who have pointed me in the right direction, I have now benefited from encountering the essential and profound contributions of Anna Julia Cooper, Frances Harper, Ida B. Wells-Barnett, Phillis Wheatley, Zora Neale Hurston, and other women to the articulation of African American political thought and history.

The most pervasive and difficult lessons I've been learning while teaching African American political thought, and more recently Race and the American Story, have come from confronting the question of the appropriateness of a white professor teaching about this topic. My introductory lecture every semester includes a candid, head-on treatment of this question. Why do I think I'm qualified to teach about African American history and political thought? That's not *my* story to tell, is it? Why do I care so much about this topic? Am I trying to indoctrinate students into a whitewashed perspective on issues of race? These questions and others are likely going through the minds of my students, and probably the minds of other faculty and administrators who hear about the course and project. I feel them going through the minds of my family and friends when I tell them what I'm teaching, writing, and thinking about. And other than the last question—to which the answer is an easy "No"—they all require lengthy and weighty discussion to address.

Hopefully I've addressed most of these types of questions for you, the reader, already. But one thing I've discovered over decades of reading and teaching is that a river metaphor can be useful in almost any situation, so I'll add that here for good measure. Each of us has our own particular stories which make up our personal identity: straight white male from the wine country, lesbian Hispanic female from Chicago, blind pianist, cancer survivor, quadriplegic singer, Islamic Persian, Chinese immigrant, Irish Catholic, and so on. These stories have static elements and fluid ones; some things attach to us or are assigned to us beyond our control, and other things are added to or subtracted from our personal identity based on our experiences and actions over time. These fluid yet structured personal stories are like streams.

When we live in community with others, our stories intersect and begin to blend to some degree with one another. My story or identity now involves or is affected by you in some way, and vice versa. Our individual streams flow into a broader communal river. This river is not the same as any of the streams, but it includes water from all of them and flows in the direction they jointly provide. When we live in community with others, parts of our stories remain particular to ourselves and parts of our stories combine to form a larger story to which we all contribute and by which we are all affected. Stephanie's story changed and grew in new directions when she came to the United States, just as mine changed when I became aware of my fellow Americans of African ancestry. Our families, friends, and communities alter the content and direction of each of our streams as they join to form larger rivers. The American story is one such communal river within which our personal streams all flow together, regardless of their points of origin.

When I teach this course, I try to join with my students in tracing out our network of personal streams and mapping their intersections with our shared river. The fact that my stream does not include the distinctive experiences associated with being African American does mean that I won't be able to shed light on this particularly important tributary of the American story. What I can do is provide an in-depth and thorough mapping of the American river that includes, in some way, input from all of its tributaries. And I can guide my students in carefully tracing the interactions of the particular streams most relevant to issues of race once they feed into our common river.

Notwithstanding my eloquence about river metaphors, however, I have often had difficulty attracting a suitably diverse student population to my classes. Many students of color are understandably wary of taking a class on race from a white professor—"what does he know?" or "what's his angle?"—and many white students simply don't care enough about the topic to devote valuable credit hours to it. There is often less viewpoint diversity in my classes than I would like, too. The type of college student interested in issues of race tends to be a liberal-progressive type of student. It can be difficult at times to avoid allowing the class discussion to degenerate into platitude-voicing or virtue-signaling. Too often students think my Socratic questioning is searching for a "right" answer rather than prodding them to think more deeply about their opinions.

I end up getting excellent students, by and large, and we end up having many great discussions. But the problem of teaching and learning about race in American history and politics is a serious one for institutions of higher education throughout the United States. Seventy-six percent of all full-time faculty members in degree-granting postsecondary institutions in the United States are white. Six percent are Black.[20] And these numbers haven't changed barely at all in the last decade. Since the early 1980s, the percentage of Black full-time faculty members has increased only in "snail-like" fashion—less than 2 percent.[21]

Courses focused on race relations in American history and politics are heavily concentrated in African American Studies departments and centers (including Black Studies, Afro-American Studies, and similarly named units). These departments emerged in the late 1960s—with the first at San Francisco State College in 1968—in response to protests and demands by Black civil rights activists. The faculty who teach in these departments and the students who take courses from them are predominantly Black. Over 70 percent of African American Studies / Black Studies degrees awarded in the United States are given to Black students; less than 10 percent are given to white students.[22]

This 7–1 ratio of Black students to white students in these programs is close to the exact opposite of the ratio of Blacks to whites in the United States population, which is about 13 percent to about 76 percent. Because of their historical origins in social protest movements and heavily African American student and faculty populations, African American / Black Studies programs largely serve to educate African American students about African American history. Meanwhile, courses outside of these programs largely serve to educate white students about an American history that often looks and sounds quite different. Black students receive one education about American history and politics, and white students receive another in most institutions of higher education in the United States.

This dynamic means that colleges and universities in the United States serve mostly to reproduce and reinforce Black/white divisions in American society at large. Many white students emerge from their college education with a desire to continue on the path of lifelong learning and go on to careers as scholars, academics, and scientists. For many African American students, this path is not even viewed as a viable or attractive option. For white American students, a college education is viewed as a social rite of passage and a springboard to continued learning and future careers. For many African American students, a college education is seen as a weapon to wield against ongoing injustice and oppression; as a tool for dismantling some of the very institutions white American college graduates are trained to uphold and preserve.

Of course a college education can be both of these things in different ways, and lifelong learning should itself be a powerful weapon against injustice and in favor of social progress. The problem is that the white students who get the one don't get the other, and the Black students who get the other don't get the one. As in American society, in American higher education we continue to segregate and pit the efforts of different groups against each other.

This is why courses like Race and the American Story—courses dealing with African American political thought, African American history, African American politics, and related topics outside of dedicated African American Studies / Black Studies departments—are so important for American higher education. Both white and Black Americans need to be rowing in the same direction when it comes to understanding what racial differences mean in American society, and what they have meant throughout American history.[23] Both white and Black Americans need to preserve and build on our shared heritage of thinking deeply about and appreciating the common humanity of people of different races. The desegregation of higher education is necessary for increasing the representation of Black and other minority faculty on college campuses, and the desegregation of courses on race in American history will be the epicenter of this process.

The Road to the Future

AM I PROGRESSIVE OR CONSERVATIVE?

In this time of heightened political and ideological polarization, many of my readers may find their preexisting allegiance to be an obstacle to sympathetically following my personal journey toward understanding and appreciating the centrality of race to the American story. Progressives won't like what I have to say about "white privilege" or "institutional racism." Conservatives will be uncomfortable with some of my commitments to "social justice," and perhaps with the whole idea of devoting a book to the issue of race. Stephanie's personal journey covers territory that is likely to be similarly unfamiliar to contemporary partisans in the United States and to take the reader down paths they don't immediately recognize as aligning with current political perspectives. Each of us has come to our opinions about race on our own—or at least independent of recent American party politics. We're both "outsiders," in ways similar and different, to the contemporary divide between progressive and conservative in the United States. People on both of these sides may initially be disappointed or confused that this book seems to resist choosing an identifiable allegiance in contemporary debates.

This is nothing new for me. Of course, there was a time in my youth when I chose the side of my parents, relatives, and friends, essentially by default.[1] My maternal grandparents were orange growers in the solidly conservative Central Valley region of California. My grandfather

Race and the American Story. Stephanie Shonekan and Adam Seagrave, Oxford University Press.
© Oxford University Press 2024. DOI: 10.1093/oso/9780197767689.003.0005

was a German immigrant who had served in the Army and instilled in his children, including my mother, the strong patriotic and conservative sentiments characteristic of European immigrants of his generation. He appreciated the opportunities and freedoms the United States had offered him and his family. He had met my Portuguese-American grandmother in France while he was in the Army and she was teaching abroad. Both from strict Roman Catholic families, they raised their children to love their country and God.

My mother strove to pass on this patriotic conservatism and religious faith to her own children. In the 1980s and 1990s, this translated clearly into political conservatism and an attachment to the Republican Party. My immediate and extended family weren't overly political, but as a kid it was clear to me that "liberal" and "Democrat" signaled "bad," and "conservative" and "Republican" signaled "good." This was never a deep feeling, though, and never really stuck with me. For a while I went along with the identification out of sheer laziness and the absence of any clear reason to repudiate it.

I was a midshipman at the US Naval Academy during the 2000 Bush vs. Gore presidential election. One of the most striking memories of this time for me occurred on the night of the election as the results were coming in. It was past lights out for us "plebes," so I was surreptitiously following the election results on a desktop computer with my roommates (this was also before smart phones, if you can imagine). Silence continued to reign across campus whenever a state was called for Gore; each time a state was called for Bush, though, Bancroft Hall erupted in cheers. The entire Academy, it seemed, was rooting for Bush. It was a comfortable moment to identify with a Republican-conservative "we."

Recently, though, one of my daughters asked me whether "we" were Republican or Democrat, and I realized how far I had come since the lazy identification of my youth and early adulthood. My answer was immediate and unequivocal: Neither. I had officially jumped ship, adrift in a sea of political and ideological independence. I can comfortably masquerade as a conservative with my conservative friends, or as a progressive liberal with my progressive liberal friends. The truth is, though, that no masquerading is required; because all of my friends and acquaintances are human beings, they are all bound to reflect and express truth at various times and in various ways. It is easy for me to try and connect with that truth whenever and however it appears.

Choosing sides when it comes to one's opinions is both lazy and treasonous to truth. Being human means cultivating a relationship with truth. Outsourcing one's opinion-formation—whether through devotion to a politician, following a celebrity obsessively on social media, or religiously listening to a talking-head on a podcast or TV show—is like allowing someone you don't know to arrange your marriage. It may seem like truth is something too extensive, complex, and evasive for any of us to get to know individually. Truth is for the smart, rich, and famous—scientists, politicians, and people on TV—to pass along to the rest of us. I have come to think, though, that it is not our possession of the truth that matters but our relationship to truth. Truth is either something we try to get to know ourselves, or it is something we don't bother searching for at all. That attempt and search is what matters—not the success or achievement of knowledge we hope will follow from it. My readers who are students of philosophy will recognize this as a core message of Plato's Socrates. My readers who are Christians will recognize this as a core message of the Gospels.

Most of us and those we know, though, will not recognize this as familiar at all. Cultivating an independent relationship to truth is arduous and often lonely work. It is just so easy and comfortable to trust others, smart people, the group, to provide opinions for us. It resonates with our innate human desire to feel as though we belong, and to identify with a closer subgroup of the human family with whom we share something more than our mere humanity. Group solidarity is important; and for rational animals like us, opinion-sharing is one of the most effective and rewarding ways of experiencing this solidarity.

There is an old saying that reflects this innate human desire: "My country, right or wrong." There is something both appealing and revolting about this saying. The attachment to country is appealing; the disregard of one's relationship to truth is revolting. Some Americans today live by that unfortunate recent variation on the maxim, "My Trumpy, right or wrong." Pro-Trump sentiment has become an exaggerated version of the opinion-outsourcing phenomenon for many, and a particular pathology of the innate human desire described above. This has contributed to the hardening and further blinding of political and ideological identities in recent years. "Make America Great Again" effectively separates or resegregates Americans into those for whom 1950s America was great and those for whom it was horrific. Conservatism and progressivism have always attracted more or less blind adherents who are more or less rigidly opposed to one another. The Trump phenomenon—which is itself only a superficial symptom of more profound cultural phenomena—has made this long-standing dynamic worse.

When one stops for a moment and reflects on ideological attachments to conservatism on the one hand or progressivism on the other, the absurdity of such attachments becomes readily apparent. Who, after all, really thinks, as a matter of principle, that things in general should be conserved? "I don't care what it is, let's keep it"—that is the pure, literal creed of a conservative, with which almost no one would agree. Conservatives only think good things should be conserved; they just think a lot of things we have are good. Hence, we should keep most of what we have. That's the conservative position.

The situation is similar for progressivism. Who really thinks, as a matter of principle, that things in general should be changed? "All change is for the better," said absolutely no one who has had any experience of human life or knowledge of human history. The opposite of the literal conservative creed is equally absurd: "I don't care what it is, let's get rid of it." It would be ridiculous to think that nothing we have is good, or that the status quo is entirely and universally bad in every way. What progressives really think is that there are many things that should be changed for the better. Because they think these things are very important, they emphasize change over stasis, movement over inertia. That's the progressive position.

Put in these ways—in other words, in the only ways a reasonable person could—conservatives and progressives don't appear to be very far apart after all. Both types think we should keep what's good and get rid of what's bad. Both think some things we have are good and some things we have are bad. What they disagree about is, partly, what counts as good and what counts as bad; and, partly, how much we currently have of each.

In the case of contemporary opinions about racial justice in the United States, the debate is less about what counts as good or bad, and more about how much we currently have of each. Most people agree on the standards of good and bad in this case, at least in general terms. More justice and equality is good, and less of these is bad. Conservative Republicans, tending to take the kind of "greatest hits" approach to American history that I've already discussed, think there is more good than bad. Progressive Democrats, focusing on everything in between and looking to important milestones still ahead, think there is more bad than good. The debate is more about quantity and emphasis rather than what counts where, or what the facts are.

In the past decade this conservative-progressive divide has widened on issues of race. In 2009—at the beginning of Obama's presidency—32 percent of Democrats viewed racism as "a big problem" in the United States, while only 18 percent of Republicans held this view.[2] In August 2017—less than a year after the end of Obama's second term and the beginning of Trump's presidency—these numbers were 76 percent for Democrats and 37 percent for Republicans. A difference of 14 percent had ballooned to a difference of 39 percent between the two parties. Looking at opinions on this question broken down by race, the divide is similar, though more constant over time: in 2009, 42 percent of Black Americans viewed racism as a "big problem" in the United States, while only 22 percent of whites did. In 2017, these numbers were 81 percent and 52 percent. Democrats are much more likely to hold the "progressive" view on the issue of racism as currently more bad than good, as are Black Americans. Republicans are much more likely to hold the "conservative" view on the issue of racism as currently more good than bad, as are white Americans.

The story of the ongoing, and widening, difference between Democrats and Republicans, and Blacks and whites, on issues of race might initially seem discouraging to someone hoping to find common ground or a way forward. This is not simply the end of the story, however. Looked at another way, these statistics are much more encouraging. In the last decade, Republicans have steadily gone from only 18 percent thinking that racism is a big problem to 37 percent; and white Americans have gone from only 22 percent to 52 percent—from less than a quarter to a majority. During the same period, Democrats and Black Americans have experienced a similar shift in their answers to this question—just one that is even more pronounced. Every group broken down in the survey—Democrat, Republican, Black, white—roughly doubled in affirmative responses to the question of whether racism is a big problem in the United States. Republicans and Democrats, Blacks and whites, have all shifted dramatically toward the progressive side of issues of race over the past decade.

This broad-based increase in pessimism about the status of racism in the United States is, ironically, also cause for optimism. Momentum behind the feeling that things aren't going well is also momentum behind the feeling that we ought to do something to bring about positive change. The fact that over a third of Republicans, and an actual majority of white Americans, recognize the problem of racism in the United States means that there is a strong political appetite for attempted solutions. More and more Americans are realizing that racism isn't a chapter in our history, but a central and defining national struggle that extends to the present day. It is far less common today than it was ten or fifteen years ago, for example, to hear disparaging complaints about someone "playing the race card." Though most conservative Republicans will still express disapproval of projects like the documentary "13th" or the *New York Times*'s 1619 Project, they don't scoff dismissively as they might have at times in the past. The mainstream conservative response to progressive efforts like these is more often a call for nuance or balance than an outright rejection.

I've seen this clearly both in personal interactions and in my role as a professor. Personally, my conversations with family members and friends who disagree with me about issues of race have been much less combative than I would have expected based on past experience. Recently, when I state certain "progressive" opinions on these topics, I'm more often greeted with a partially puzzled but partially thoughtful silence than with an immediate counterargument. And when I explain my opinions or give arguments for them, I get the sense that even if my interlocutor doesn't agree with me, she doesn't disagree with me either. Racial justice still isn't a priority issue for a large majority of Americans, and particularly for white Americans. The old Stephen Douglas "care not" policy is still prevalent. But a clear majority of Americans now see ongoing racial injustices as a problem; and seeing something as a problem is a crucial step on the way to caring about solving it.

I've witnessed similar trends in my interaction with faculty colleagues as well as with students. I recently wrote a short article for a conservative website that defended the *New York Times'* 1619 Project against conservative critics. The first positive sign was that the website immediately accepted the article for publication despite its critical stance toward prominent members of the website's primary audience. My conservative colleagues and friends read the article and, though some expressed clear disagreements with my interpretation of the controversy, many also expressed approval of its charitable approach to the 1619 Project authors. It wasn't considered outlandish or ridiculous for a white academic who studies American political thought and history to publish views sympathetic to those of Black advocates for racial justice.

Even over the last five years the attitudes and opinions of my students have migrated noticeably toward increasing sympathy with causes of racial justice. I used to have a substantial number of conservative students who would voice the standard old-school conservative, sanitized, naive outlook on issues of race: slavery was bad, but thanks to our Founders and Lincoln it's over and done with now. Over the last few years, none of my conservative-leaning students have evidenced holding such a view. Now, my more conservative students will agree wholeheartedly with statements about the ongoing legacies of slavery, segregation, and discrimination. Their conservative leanings express themselves in terms of drawing attention to the positive contributions of American founders such as Thomas Jefferson, or of classic American documents such as the Declaration of Independence or the Constitution. Conservative Republican college students today take a "both-and" approach to the topic of racial justice— both attention to ongoing injustices and appreciation for American founding principles and history.

The Race and the American Story course syllabus reinforces this promising trend toward a consensus approach to ongoing issues of racial justice. In the course we read a chapter from Alexis de Tocqueville's *Democracy in America*—a generally very positive, exceptionalist account of American politics and history—in which he clearly explains the uniqueness of American-style race-based chattel slavery and highlights the unique problems associated with the institution. In classic Tocquevillian style, he argues with an uncanny counterintuitive prescience that the problems associated with American slavery will only get worse and more difficult to deal with after legal abolition than before. We read Frederick Douglass, who in the same brilliant speech praises the authors of the Declaration of Independence and Constitution to the heavens and excoriates the dominant "moral blindness" of the American people in failing to recognize and rectify racial injustices. We read Phillis Wheatley, Frances Harper, W. E. B. DuBois, Zora Neale Hurston, and others who defy characterization as either progressive or conservative on the contemporary spectrum.

Reading these great and courageous minds from America's past clearly reveals that polarization of political opinions about race in America is an aberration. We might be hardwired as human beings to certain racist tendencies; the tendency of white Americans to "perceive and receive" Black Americans in exclusionary and unjust ways is, as Stephanie's experience clearly shows, as alive and well today as it ever was. These tendencies have been powerfully reinforced for Americans by the history of racist enslavement and segregation in the United States. This continuing racism in social dynamics and personal interactions sits uneasily with a contrary kind of American hardwiring: the conviction most Americans feel for the principles of freedom and equality. This conviction has led—circuitously and through fits and starts, to be sure—to the broad cultural and legal condemnation of racism reflected in the political opinions expressed by most Americans across the political spectrum today. The same people who might "cancel" Stephanie socially are likely to hold more progressive opinions on racial issues than their parents or grandparents did. Human culture, like individual human beings, is complicated; the "better angels" (to quote Lincoln) always coexist with worse ones. In the United States, the gap between these has always been remarkably pronounced.

It was because of this enormous gap that the situation before the Civil War was inherently volatile and unsustainable, like dancing with a bottle of nitroglycerin. There is something profoundly comforting about belonging to a group defined in opposition to another group—a human tendency that leads naturally to racism in the right circumstances. In the American case, though, this group definition and distinction by race ran head-on into moral convictions about human equality and rights that form a profound component of American identity. As in the memorable Lee Greenwood song, freedom is one of the most profound sources of American patriotism. Take that away—which is literally what slavery and its legacies do—and there isn't much left to be proud of. In American history, our human nature has sometimes fought powerfully against our deepest convictions as Americans. The Civil War was an extreme example of the combustible nature of this internal conflict. The Civil Rights struggles in the mid-twentieth century were another. In both cases, American moral principles of freedom and justice were reaffirmed and better applied. Still, though, people like Stephanie are justifiably afraid for their sons; and no amount of political consensus and moral conviction has yet found a way to excise these forms of racism from our American society.

* * *

OF MONUMENTS AND MEMORIES

Civil war and secession memories remain deeply rooted in the consciousness of a people for centuries. Stories about what was done to one group by another, about why people felt the need to challenge the concept of the nation-state are passed down from generation to generation. We are never quite rid of these enduring bits of memory. Growing up in Nigeria, I heard stories of the Biafran war, about how my father's people—the Igbo—were mistreated by the rest of the country. Even though this war has been over for over fifty years, the country continues to experience the echoes of those three tragic years from 1967 to 1970. As Nigeria stood on the verge of a presidential election in 2023, one heard whispers that Nigeria will never allow an Igbo man to be president. These whispers signify how our current reality is tightly woven into our historical memory. The same is true here in the United States. Nationalistic songs like Lee Greenwood's "God Bless the USA," which Adam refers to, are perceived one way or the other, depending on what side one's ancestors stood during the US Civil War, or on the narratives that have been passed down in families through the generations. Which God are we referring to here—the blond, blue-eyed God? When the lyrics get to the line "I'm proud to be an American where at least I know I'm free," what does freedom mean? Were George Floyd, Trayvon Martin, Tamir Rice, Rekia Boyd, and Eric Garner truly free? Is it really full freedom if I have to worry about my children being stopped by the police simply because they are Black? Are we a liberated society if a white woman has to ask the receptionist if she would be safe with my husband in his office? These instances, microaggressions, happen all the time, everyday across America. Taking nothing away from the gratitude conveyed in songs like this to the military for defending the sovereignty of the nation, we can still ask questions about what full freedom means within the borders of the United States. And these questions are embedded in the memory of this nation.

Often, memories are contained in statues and monuments. At the University of Missouri, students were up in arms about a bronze statue that sits on the quad. It is a seated statue of Thomas Jefferson, whose plans for the University of Virginia were in part replicated to establish the University of Missouri. This was also the first university (established in 1839) in the Louisiana Purchase territory. Next to the statue, which was donated to the university in 2001, sits a granite obelisk, Jefferson's original grave marker, with a replica epitaph to Thomas Jefferson that reads: "Here was buried Thomas Jefferson, Author of the Declaration of American Independence, of the Statute of Virginia for religious freedom & Father of the University of Virginia." This epitaph was in his own words. He meant future generations to remember his work at the dawn of the birth of the country, that he authored the declaration, the notion of freedom (of religion and speech), and the fact that he established the University of Virginia. On this epitaph we are reminded of the Founder's attention to intellectual progress, humanistic freedom, and a reverence for God. This is all good and worthy of remembrance. Although he didn't participate in the work of the Constitutional Convention, his interpretation of the Constitution's meaning and importance is also illustrious and memorialized in volumes, films, and literature.

According to Frederick Douglass: "the Constitution of the United States, standing alone, and construed *only* in the light of its letter, without reference to the opinions of the men who framed and adopted it, or to the uniform, universal and undeviating practice of the nation under it, from the time of its adoption until now, is not a pro-slavery instrument."[3] But, like everything else, sociologically speaking, we do have to consider and reference the opinions of the men who framed and adopted it. As human beings, we do not live an "only" existence. Instead, we live lives that are interwoven, interlocked, surrounded by contexts and contents that shape how we choose to live and think. As Audre Lorde wrote, "There is no such thing as a single-issue struggle because we do not live single-issue lives."[4] I am not simply a professor. I am a Black woman, a Black mother, half Nigerian, half Trinidadian, and so on. All this means that my decisions and choices are a composite product of the various panes of my mosaic identity.

So we must also consider Jefferson's legacy from all angles of American citizenship. For instance, when we look back at the postindependent Nigeria and the unrest and tension that bubbled up to the surface soon after independence, we cannot take the words of Biafran leader Ojukwu and apply it to all Nigerians. We have to consider what those words meant to and for the Biafrans in contrast to other Nigerians. The difference in these perceptions laid the foundation for the bitter and deadly civil war I mentioned above. For the same reasons, it behooves us in the 2020s to look back even further, to the founding of the United States, to assess to whom and for whom the ideals etched into the constitution were directed. To understand why so many Black students have protested the existence of the statue on the quad since it got there, we must go back to the stories they were told, by their parents and grandparents, stories that were handed down from one generation to the next, across the expanse of time from 1619, through emancipation, reconstruction, the Jim Crow era, civil rights era, through the crack epidemic and the US justice system that treated this not as a health epidemic (as the opioid crisis is treated) but as criminal pathology, to the Black Lives Matter era. These stories have traveled like folklore, but they are an uncontestable and documented part of American history.[5] I am always mindful of the attentiveness to the different angles from which we view history.[6] As the story goes, when Christopher Columbus put his telescope up and sighted the West Indies, he thought he was looking at East India. It was only when he landed that he realized he was mistaken. Yes, he saw a mass of land, but he did not have the technology to see all angles. We still struggle for that technology today.

Black students at Mizzou have a unique and particular angle from which to view the statue. Some administrators and some donors have a different angle. The fundamental question remains this: Was the Declaration of Independence written for all Americans? For whom was the Constitution written? With the full understanding that this document was ratified at a time when the country was deep in the throes of an inhumane slavery system, scholars have leafed through it with skepticism and hope. Even the great Frederick Douglass struggled with this question, viewing it first as a proslavery document and later shifting his position, his angle, (perhaps his strategy?) to view it as an antislavery document.[7] While it is good to view a document and judge it on its own merits, it is also natural as human beings to consider the authors of the document and determine the full picture of its meaning. So, in the Declaration of Independence (1776), "all men are created equal" sounds wonderful if I replace "men" with "people" and if I dismiss the 3/5 clause that comes later in the Constitution (1789). When I look at the preamble of the Constitution, I have to ask myself who "We the people" are. My mind has to do a few contortions to settle on the beauty of these ideals. As an immigrant, I wonder if I am included, but I just arrived! What are the questions on the minds of our Black students at universities like Mizzou? Were their ancestors, who were here at the time of ratification, who were viewed as taxable property and not as full human beings, were they on the minds of the founders when they wrote "we the people"? These are entirely reasonable questions. One can sing along to the song "I Believe I Can Fly" because one loves the melody and lyrics of the song and the *Space Jam* movie, yet question the morality and legacy of R. Kelly. At its composition, it was brilliant, but from what we now know about the songwriter, we can speculate on who he meant this song for. He could fly, but what about the young women he preyed on? Keep in mind that the Black students at Mizzou were not directly quarreling with the ideals of the constitution nor its notions of freedom. They were focused on the R. Kelly of the American Constitutional order.

Before we approach the hallowed person of Thomas Jefferson, I want to focus for a moment on three other well-known founders of nations and movements: Robert Mugabe of Zimbabwe, Mahatma Gandhi of India, and Aung San Suu Kyi of Myanmar. Mugabe fought diligently to overthrow the oppressive white Rhodesian government. While most other African countries gained independence in the 1950s and 1960s, Zimbabwe had to wait until 1980 to overcome the British colonizers. At the birth of that new nation, as the Union Jack was lowered and as the Zimbabwean flag was lifted, Mugabe was seen as a hero of the people, distinguished among African and world leaders.

Similarly, Gandhi's legacy for facing off against the British in India is almost uncontested. The African American civil rights leaders were inspired by his philosophies of nonviolent resistance and used these in the 1950s and 1960s to apprehend the social injustice of Jim Crow laws. They studied Gandhian strategy and adopted his teachings. Aung San Suu Kyi served fifteen years under house arrest for challenging the military regime of Burma/Myanmar. For her stoic commitment to freedom for her people, she was awarded the Nobel Peace Prize in 1991. She was known as one of the "Children of Gandhi."

Each of these world leaders had their bright day in the sun of our collective esteem. However, when different angles are approached, we begin to see that they are not as worthy of the acclaim and prizes as we once thought. As he grew in power, Mugabe became more emboldened to clutch to that power like a string of precious pearls. He snuffed out his opposition and adopted policies that had a fundamental effect on the masses, the most powerless. Last year, at the University of Ghana, a statue of Gandhi was lowered as a result of renewed revelations of his racism.[8] Apparently, when he was working in South Africa, he had advocated for Indians with the stipulation that they must not be treated as Black South Africans were. There is no way of knowing this fact that does not result in a racist Gandhi. And finally, we now know that Aung San Suu Kyi has turned away from (or instigated?) the violent terrorism against millions of Rohingya Muslims and refugees in Myanmar. As we consider these three world leaders from all angles, we can reassess the fit of their crowns. We don't have to be a poor Zimbabwean, a Black South African, or a Rohingya Muslim to admit that there are shadows over the legacies of Mugabe, Gandhi, and Aung San Suu Kyi. The sun has set on their legacies.

And so we approach Thomas Jefferson in the same way. This is not one of those times when we can send certain dictators or war criminals to the international courts but refuse to even consider the courts for other generals, secretaries of defense, and presidents in the United States who have used false justifications for going to war with countries. If we can agree to treat all world leaders the same way, let us look at the attitude and beliefs of Thomas Jefferson as well.[9] In the last few years, historians like Annette Gordon-Reed have uncovered research that points to Jefferson's sexual relationship with enslaved Sally Hemings. Any reading of this relationship as in any way romantic is dishonest when one considers her age of fourteen to his forty-four, and the power Jefferson had over Hemings as her owner and the owner of her relatives and children. This was sexual violence. Apart from the Sally Hemings case, we have his own words about Black people to go on. In his *Notes on the State of Virginia* (1785), he waxes on about his pseudoscientific views of Black folks:

> The difference is fixed in nature, and is as real as if its seat and cause were better known to us. And is this difference of no importance? Is it not the foundation of a greater or less share of beauty in the two races? Are not the fine mixtures of red and white, the expressions of

every passion by greater or less suffusions of color in the one, preferable to that eternal monotony, which reigns in the countenances, that
immoveable veil of Black which covers all the emotions of the other
race? Add to these, flowing hair, a more elegant symmetry of form,
their own judgment in favor of the whites, declared by their preference of them, as uniformly as is the preference of the orangutan for
the Black women over those of his own species. The circumstance
of superior beauty, is thought worthy attention in the propagation
of our horses, dogs, and other domestic animals; why not in that of
man? . . . they seem to require less sleep. A Black, after hard labor
through the day, will be induced by the slightest amusements to sit
up till midnight, or later, though knowing he must be out with the
first dawn of the morning. They are at least as brave, and more adven-
turesome. But this may perhaps proceed from a want of forethought,
which prevents their seeing a danger till it be present. When present,
they do not go through it with more coolness or steadiness than the
whites. They are more ardent after their female: but love seems with
them to be more an eager desire, than a tender delicate mixture of
sentiment and sensation. Their griefs are transient. Those numberless
afflictions, which render it doubtful whether heaven has given life to
us in mercy or in wrath, are less felt, and sooner forgotten with them.
In general, their existence appears to participate more of sensation
than reflection. . . . Comparing them by their faculties of memory,
reason, and imagination, it appears to me, that in memory they are
equal to the whites; in reason much inferior, as I think one [Black]
could scarcely be found capable of tracing and comprehending the
investigations of Euclid; and that in imagination they are dull, taste-
less, and anomalous. It would be unfair to follow them to Africa for
this investigation. We will consider them here, on the same stage
with the whites . . .

    . . . the facts are not apocryphal on which a judgment is to be
formed. It will be right to make great allowances for the difference
of condition, of education, of conversation, of the sphere in which
they move. Many millions of them have been brought to, and born

in America. Most of them indeed have been confined to tillage, to their own homes, and their own society: yet many have been so situated, that they might have availed themselves of the conversation of their masters; many have been brought up to the handicraft arts, and from that circumstance have always been associated with the whites. Some have been liberally educated, and all have lived in countries where the arts and sciences are cultivated to a considerable degree, and have had before their eyes samples of the best works from abroad. The Indians, with no advantages of this kind, will often carve figures on their pipes not destitute of design and merit. They will crayon out an animal, a plant, or a country, so as to prove the existence of a germ in their minds which only wants cultivation. They astonish you with strokes of the most sublime oratory; such as prove their reason and sentiment strong, their imagination glowing and elevated. But never yet could I find that a Black had uttered a thought above the level of plain narration; never see even an elementary trait of painting or sculpture. In music they are more generally gifted than the whites with accurate ears fortune and time. . . . Whether they will be equal to the composition of a more extensive run of melody, or of complicated harmony, is yet to be proved. Misery is often the parent of the most affecting touches in poetry.—Among the Blacks is misery enough, God knows, but no poetry.

. . . To our reproach it must be said, that though for a century and a half we have had under our eyes the races of Black and of red men, they have never yet been viewed by us as subjects of natural history. I advance it therefore as a suspicion only, that the Blacks, whether originally a distinct race, or made distinct by time and circumstances, are inferior to the whites in the endowments both of body and mind. It is not against experience to suppose, that different species of the same genus, or varieties of the same species, may possess different qualifications.

Jefferson insists here that there is indeed a significant difference between Black and white folks, and that ultimately, white people are the superior race. The people he writes about here are the ancestors of our Black students on campus. They are linked by a bloodline through history. Why would we expect them to be comfortable walking on a campus that reveres this writer? Why would we expect the Rohingya Muslims to calmly behold a statue of Ang San Suu Kyi when she could have prevented thousands of cases of violence that led to death and homelessness? The same question can be asked of statues of Mugabe and Gandhi. The United States will indeed be great when it can approach all angles, settle on more truths, and commit to a more just future.

* * *

NATURAL RIGHTS

How does our assessment of Jefferson the man, and the angles of perspective on memorializing this man through monuments, affect our assessment of the documents he authored and the ideas he held? Some of these ideas, such as those expressed with grotesque clarity in the *Notes on the State of Virginia*, were blatantly racist. Others, such as those expressed in his draft of the Declaration of Independence, were blatantly antiracist. Of these latter, the one with the most lasting positive legacy has been the idea of natural rights—an idea that was very much "in the air" at the time of the American Revolution. It was so much in the air, in fact, that Jefferson claimed the expression of natural rights in the Declaration of Independence was really not his idea at all, but rather an "expression of the American mind." Our ideas of rights today are related to Jefferson's Revolutionary idea of natural rights but are not identical to it. Both are connected to human freedom, dignity, and equality, but not by identical bonds. Understanding how the two differ—what "nature" adds to the equation, and what its subtraction removes—is crucial to appreciating the ideals of an era, and of a generation, whose racist practices we abhor.

Natural rights are the rights of human nature. They are the rights that all human beings possess by virtue of being human, and because of the essential nature that all human beings share. They can be internationally recognized, as they are in documents like the Universal Declaration of Human Rights, but this recognition is not what gives them their existence. A human being sitting on a rock, naked and alone, in the middle of the ocean possesses these rights equally with King Charles on her throne in Buckingham Palace.

According to the philosophical tradition that originated with John Locke in the seventeenth century, was carried forward in one way by Hegel, and then was applied to the African American experience by W. E. B. Du Bois, natural rights have to do with the structure of human self-awareness. Human nature is reflective in ways that do not appear to be shared by the rest of animal and vegetable nature. Human beings can think and talk about themselves. Lebron James can refer to himself in the third person. What is significant about this? The ability to think and speak of oneself in the third person—as an object—means that a human being's experience is both immediate, as it is with all animals, and also subsequently mediated through awareness and conscious thought. We human beings are not only what we are, but also what we think about ourselves.

This means, among other interesting things, that human beings are naturally self-creative. The natural human capacity for self-awareness also entails a structure and process through which people naturally superimpose a narrative idea of themselves on top of their bare experiences. After enjoying a roller coaster ride we don't just leave it there; we become someone who likes roller coasters, and we integrate that reflective fact into our identity. Innumerable experiences, large and small, become integrated into our identity in the same way, constantly and unavoidably, over time throughout our lives. We naturally "own" our experiences, just as when someone "owns" something they said or did by admitting it to others.

This natural human self-ownership is what Locke meant by natural rights. Hegel elaborated on Locke's idea by highlighting the role that others can play in the process of constructive self-narratives. Other people can recognize and confirm our own inner portrayal of ourselves, or they can contradict and deny it. Human societies can have a powerful effect on the self-understanding of the people who live within them.

Du Bois applied this insight to his analysis of African American history in *The Souls of Black Folk*. According to Du Bois, African Americans are often forced into a kind of "double-consciousness" by a "veil" of racism that interrupts and distorts their natural human process of self-awareness. African Americans are prevented from seeing themselves as they really are by the racism of American society. The experience of being "Black" in the United States is significantly different from the experience of skin color in Nigeria or other countries. African Americans are treated differently, and have a different self-conscious identity, than Africans in America, as Stephanie's experience clearly attests. Just as institutionalized, legal slavery prevented African Americans from owning themselves in a material sense, so racism, discrimination, and segregation prevented African Americans from fully owning themselves in a psychological sense. The latter crime may have been even more evil and insidious than the first.

Du Bois didn't refer to this psychological violence in terms of a violation of natural rights because he didn't explicitly connect his own psychological analysis to the analysis John Locke had presented centuries earlier. Though Du Bois clearly saw the relationship between his account of African American experience and the principles of the Declaration of Independence, he lived in the midst of a time when the idea of natural rights was all but forgotten in the United States. This period of forgetfulness, coinciding almost exactly with the period of Du Bois's own lifetime, also coincided—not coincidentally—with a prolonged dark age for African American civil rights following the brief moment of hope represented by the Civil War amendments and the early years of Reconstruction.

RACISM BETWEEN THE 60S

Expressions of racism have evolved significantly over the course of American history. At the beginning, interpersonal or social expressions of racism were conditioned to some extent by the legal institution of slavery. As the great nineteenth-century French commentator Alexis de

Tocqueville opined in *Democracy in America*, the legal barrier of slavery sometimes appeared to lessen the need for other, additional expressions of racism on top of this primary, horrific one of enslavement. Rigid legal hierarchy creates a sort of comfort zone for those on the higher end of the scale that can discourage additional expressions of disdain or animosity. Think, for example, of the pleasant lord/lady–servant dynamic represented in *Downton Abbey*. Injustice on the part of the system sometimes relieves the motivation for further injustice on the part of the individuals who benefit from it.

The 13th Amendment abolished the legal barrier of slavery, and in doing so inaugurated a new era of more obvious and open expressions of racism on the part of individuals and groups in society. Once the legal system relinquished its role of upholding racial hierarchy, individual people felt the need to take on this task themselves. In a perverse example of the libertarian position, the retreat of government created an opening for an invigoration of individual initiative and civil society. This era reached its gruesome peak in the widespread practice of lynching. Ida Wells meticulously documented more than five hundred cases of the lynching of Black Americans during the five-year period from 1896 to 1900 alone; likely only a small fraction of the total number that occurred in the post-Reconstruction era.[10] As the law became less racist, individuals in civil society became more racist.

The period that followed the initial promise and then failure of Reconstruction was marked by widespread American social and political "ignore-ance" regarding racial justice, punctuated by terrible public acts of violence against African Americans. This was the period—roughly 1900 to 1965—that renowned political scientist Robert Putnam glowingly referred to as the "We" period in a recent public talk hosted at ASU. This period saw a steep and constant increase in volunteerism and membership in all sorts of organizations. Before people began "*Bowling Alone*" in the late 1960s, they had cheerfully bowled together at incredible rates for decades before. The "Baby Boom" generation was born as the marriage rate skyrocketed. Viewed from the perspective of white society, American democracy was doing swell. Everything seemed "great" for white Americans.

Meanwhile, beyond the white American island, the Great Migration was occurring as Black Americans living in the South fled northward in incredible numbers. About 6 million Black Americans—nearly half of the Black population in the South—moved during this time. And they didn't move so they could join more bowling leagues with their white friends; they moved so they could escape oppressive state regimes. They were refugees from one part of the United States seeking asylum in another. Du Bois himself despaired of ever achieving equal civil rights in the United States and lived his final years in Ghana.[11]

The incredible importance of segregation to the psyche of white Americans in the twentieth century can readily be seen in the reactions to the Supreme Court's 1954 decision in *Brown v. Board of Education*.[12] There was such an appetite for massive resistance by white Southerners that a US Senator from Virginia actually led a campaign uncreatively called "Massive Resistance." The governor of Arkansas at the time, Orval Faubus—whose very name sounds like it might be a mistake—called out the state National Guard to prevent Black students from attending high school in Little Rock. President Eisenhower had to deploy federal troops to literally force Arkansas to allow its schools to be desegregated. It took one of the best Civil War reenactments ever produced (minus the actual shooting, thankfully) to get white Americans in Arkansas to allow nine Black students to attend one of their schools. A six-year-old Black girl named Ruby Bridges needed to be escorted to school by four federal marshals for protection from mobs of protestors. That needs some time to really sink in: a six-year-old girl trying to go to school needed protection from potentially violent, screaming protestors. In the United States, fairly recently.

The less obvious lesson to be drawn from these events is the crucial role that legal segregation had played in the preceding decades. Legal segregation wasn't merely a divisive political issue; it was a way of being for Southern white communities. It wasn't controversial; it was existential. As psychologists would tell us, the existence of a vibrant "we" usually depends upon the coexistence of an excluded "them." Just as patriotism is

often buoyed by conflict with foreign nations, group solidarity within nations can be powerfully supported by the marginalization of other groups.
Desegregation in the 1950s and civil rights in the 1960s coincided with the
beginning of the decline of community in the United States at least partly
because white Americans chose to retreat from their communities rather
than widen them to include Black Americans.[13]

Very few white Americans have ever heard of what Black Americans
were doing between *Plessy v. Ferguson* in 1896 and *Brown v. Board* in 1954.
We learn about Lincoln and the abolition of slavery, and then about Martin
Luther King Jr. and the civil rights movement. This gap in our knowledge
contributes to the temptation to dismiss racial grievances as complaining
or playing the victim. As far as white Americans are generally concerned,
the two crucial moments in African American history are the abolition of
slavery and the achievement of equal civil rights. Both of these are positive, even triumphal moments. This is a happy story, right? Why do many
Black Americans decline to focus on these particular, triumphal moments
in the same way? The answer is simple: because they know too well all of
the moments in between, and because they have ordinary experiences of
racism—like being called the N word while walking down the street, or
being questioned by police because they "match a description" or "look
suspicious"—that very few white Americans ever hear about. Ignorance,
and "ignore-ance," is bliss.

The positive legal milestones that are particularly impressive to white
Americans are also misleading because of their counterintuitive social and
individual-level effects: as Tocqueville noticed, the lifting of legal barriers
to equality and justice often directly stimulates the imposition of new social and individual-level barriers to equality and justice. Inequality and
injustice don't disappear with the abolition of their legal manifestation,
they just go underground and become embedded deeper in the fabric of
society. This is particularly the case when inequality and injustice exist
along clearly defined and visible racial lines. The distinctions previously
imposed by law seem to be echoed and affirmed by the distinctions naturally drawn by our sense of sight.

EQUALITY AND FREEDOM, AMERICAN STYLE

There was nothing inevitable about the progress we have achieved on racial justice since the time of the American Founding, or since the time of the civil rights movement after the long dark ages in the century between the 'ß60s. This progress was brought about through the contingent and heroic efforts of both Black and white Americans. There was, though, a way in which these efforts were powerfully supported by sources of inspiration from within American political thought and history. This inspiration has been like a wave that can, under the right guidance and application, supply the national momentum for progress.

We mean something more specific and concrete here than Martin Luther King Jr.'s famous statement that "the arc of the moral universe is long, but it bends towards justice." We also mean something different from Tocqueville's account of the inevitable progress of equality over time through human history, or Hegel's views about the inexorable march of the Idea of Freedom in human consciousness over time. All of these grander visions of historical progress may be right, but they are vague, general, eschatological observations of limited relevance to understanding and interpreting particular historical trends, events, or peoples.

The solid, identifiable, inspirational momentum particular to American history and politics is not the grand worldwide momentum of equality or freedom, but a more particular and definite expression of it. It is the momentum of an idea rather than a feeling or desire, a momentum of conviction rather than emotion. This is the idea that used to be expressed in terms of "natural rights." Beginning in the mid-nineteenth century, with the growth of industrialization and urbanization accompanying new scientific attitudes toward nature, the language of "natural rights" was largely abandoned. The idea was then resurrected in the twentieth century in terms of "human rights," reflecting the more abstract cosmopolitanism of the United Nations in the aftermath of World War II.[14] In the time since, "human rights" have coexisted alongside similar expressions of "fundamental" or "basic" rights. The core idea in all of these expressions is that of individual human dignity or worth. This idea adds to those of justice, equality, or freedom by further specifying the outlines of these concepts in their application to human societies and public policies. Equality means equal innate human dignity. Justice means treating individuals in accordance with their innate human dignity. Freedom means the ability to act in keeping with one's innate human dignity.

Viewing American history through this lens or from this particular angle—as a chronicle of the momentum of a conviction—reveals why issues of racial justice have always occupied a central place in American politics. In the face of this conviction about human dignity, the moral wrongness of slavery was obvious, even to many of those—like Thomas Jefferson—who had the most incentive to blind themselves to it. The American conviction functioned like 3D glasses when it came to race-based slavery, highlighting the vast expanse between the one and the other. As Frederick Douglass said, "There is not a man beneath the canopy of heaven who does not know that slavery is wrong for him."[15] But the American conviction takes this one step further, making it abundantly clear that slavery is wrong not only for oneself but also for any other human being. Despite the sophisms and rhetorical gymnastics employed by many Southerners before the Civil War to establish the subhumanity of African Americans, or the biblical justification of race-based slavery, the application of the American conviction to the institution of slavery by Abraham Lincoln, Frederick Douglass, and many others was simply too compelling to be finally resisted. The conservation of American identity— a kind of "conservatism," however radical and crusading—demanded it.

A similar point can be made about the moral wrongness of lynching— a practice closely connected in American history to the preceding institution of race-based slavery. The brutal spectacle of extrajudicial killing by mobs of vigilantes, like the practice of forced enslavement, leaps out from the American landscape with 3D clarity when viewed through the lens of the American conviction. The inclinations of human nature lead us in multiple and contrary directions—revulsion at inhuman brutality coupled with curiosity and interest—but the addition of principled conviction inevitably tips the scale. As in the case of slavery, lynching is a practice that can't stand against the particular momentum of American history. Both are so clearly

opposed to the American conviction of human dignity that they are incapable of stable coexistence with it. The recent passage of the Emmett Till
Anti-lynching Act in the House of Representatives by a 410–4 vote provides
clear support for this point—despite its inexcusable tardiness in coming.[16]

The fact that this antilynching bill received near-unanimous support in
a political context generally characterized by incredibly high levels of parti-
sanship and ideological polarization between conservatives and progressives
is telling. It further witnesses the point made above regarding our current
historical moment and its ripeness for a new wave of progress on issues of
racial justice. Even racial justice issues with a less obvious connection to the
legacy of slavery, such as criminal justice reform, are experiencing similarly
broad based support. According to a 2017 poll released by the American Civil
Liberties Union, 91 percent of Americans say the criminal justice system has
problems that need to be fixed. Majorities of Americans in every partisan
and major ideological grouping support a variety of changes to the criminal justice system geared toward reducing prison populations, eliminating
mandatory minimum sentencing, and other changes. Only one in three
Americans polled agree that Black people are treated fairly by the criminal
justice system.[17] Despite ongoing controversy over points of priority and emphasis, the seriousness of past injustices including slavery and lynching, and
the reality of slavery's ongoing legacies for Black Americans today are relatively uncontroversial. There is reason to hope that this time around we can
make significant progress on issues of racial justice without the need for a
Civil War, a civil rights social movement, or the intervention of the Supreme
Court. If this progress can be achieved politically and through the democratic legislative process, it will be a major step forward for the American
experiment.[18]

RACIAL JUSTICE VS. OTHER SOCIAL
JUSTICE MOVEMENTS

Social justice movements in the United States have not only focused on
race. But racial justice has been a critical need since the beginning of this

country's founding in the most dramatic and urgent ways. The fight for racial justice has inspired other social justice movements, such as indigenous sovereignty, women's rights, immigration rights, and environmental justice. While other scholars can illuminate the history and verity of these movements, we remain steadfast in our focus on the status and importance of the rights of Black people—against the institution of enslavement, legal segregation, historical and modern-day lynching, or other historically race-based injustices in the United States.

While Americans are divided on other social justice movements, there seems to be a gaining of ground in public opinion regarding African American rights movements. A nationwide Gallup poll in 1964 found that support for the Civil Rights Act of that same year stood at 58 percent, with only 31 percent expressing disapproval of the bill. In 1965, another Gallup poll found that 76 percent of Americans supported a proposed equal voting rights law. Two months after the march for voting rights in Selma, Alabama, in 1965, a Pew Center survey found that 48 percent of Americans sided with the civil rights groups over the state of Alabama while only 21 percent sided with the state. Among white Americans alone, support for the civil rights groups was more than double support for the state.[19] Amid significant disagreements over civil rights strategy as well as continuing and even intensifying racism, a clear supermajority of Americans in the mid-1960s agreed on the need to secure equal civil rights for African Americans.

The conclusion from these numbers is clear: While there are obvious similarities between racism against African Americans and discrimination against other marginalized groups, and while they all have similar effects with respect to social marginalization, exclusion from opportunities, and individual-level violence, most Americans recognize that there are also obvious differences between African American rights issues and those of others in the United States.

Race in the United States is attached to biological heredity, it is visually identified, and it is associated directly with centuries-long legal enslavement, legal segregation, and systematic exemption from the protection of law. There are currently around 45 million Black Americans in the United States.[20] As of 2013, nearly 9 percent of these individuals were, like Stephanie, immigrants—a significant increase from a total of just over 3 percent in 1980.[21] This recent immigration is the largest wave of Black immigration to the United States in history. Even after this wave of immigration, only about 3 percent of Black Americans self-identified as being descended from recent immigrants to the United States in 2010.[22]

Of these recent immigrants and their descendants, moreover, a large majority are from the Caribbean. Although it is difficult to estimate with precision, this means that of the hundreds of millions of Black Americans who have lived in the United States (or what would become the United States) since the early seventeenth century, the vast majority—likely well over 90 percent—are directly descended from people forcibly brought across the Atlantic into chattel enslavement solely on the basis of their race.

The institution of American slavery powerfully shaped the American Founding, even if the picture of this influence is more complex than the initial, uncorrected version of the "1619 Project" would have it. The Civil War, which still stands as the most destructive, widespread, and disruptive event in American history—by far—was caused primarily and fundamentally by slavery.[23] The institutional effects of the Civil War in terms of the federal balance and executive power in particular have been far reaching and permanent. The 14th Amendment, initially adopted specifically to secure the rule of law and civil rights for formerly enslaved African Americans, has been the Constitutional basis for rights expansion across all dimensions since the middle of the twentieth century.[24] Movements for African American rights gave us Abraham Lincoln and Martin Luther King Jr., the closest instances of consensus political heroes in American history since the Founding, and the two most internationally renowned symbols of American identity abroad.

African American rights movements—the abolition movement for natural rights against enslavement, and then the movements for civil and political rights since—have defined American history. Not only African American history, but American history. As the "1619 Project" suggests, and as many prominent Americans from John Quincy Adams to Frederick Douglass to Abraham Lincoln to W. E. B. Du Bois to Martin Luther King

Jr. have affirmed, African American rights movements have been an even more dramatic and significant application of American political principles than was the American Revolution itself. As Du Bois said at the turn of the twentieth century, "there are to-day no truer exponents of the pure human spirit of the Declaration of Independence than the American Negroes."[25] Regardless of one's position on other issues of rights extension in the United States, it is simply a historical and commonsensical fact that the struggle for African American civil and natural rights has been a unique one in American history. This fact is reflected in the level of consensus that is present around issues of African American civil rights, in contrast to the persistent controversy surrounding other issues of rights extension in the United States

It is for these reasons that the Race and the American Story project has stubbornly refused to amend its mission by incorporating elements of other rights movements in the United States or around the world. Progress on racial justice depends on maintaining this focus; and progress in other dimensions of natural human rights will likely be built on this foundation as well. The American conviction about human dignity and worth should speak with a megaphone when it comes to struggles for racial justice in American history. When it comes to other controversies over rights in the United States, it definitely hems and haws. Each category of injustice must be attended to in unique approaches that highlight the character of the particular injustice. For racial injustice we go back to the founding and trace the pathologies of racism still visible in our society. This would be an appropriate and effective strategy for pursuing stable consensus with respect to ongoing questions of rights extension in the United States. But there are obvious complications. We want to emphasize that identities are never as clean-cut as Black and white. As Stephanie focuses on race, her peculiar personal history means that she also deals with at least two other identity strikes—being a woman and being an immigrant. There are therefore layered and interlocking aspects of injustice. Legal scholar Kimberlé Crenshaw calls this phenomenon "intersectionality," and scholars like bell hooks and Patricia Hill Collins introduced the concept of Black feminist thought to remind us that race is compounded by other marginal parts of their identities. Our Race and the American Story course takes this into consideration by insisting on including Black women like Phillis Wheatley, Anna Julia Cooper, Ida B. Wells, and Zora Neale Hurston.

A WAY FORWARD

Progress on racial justice has been significantly hindered since the civil rights movement. There are competing calls on our attention, and the clouds of historical memory continue to hover over the dawn of the next generation of Americans. Contemporary political liberals tend to appeal to disembodied, vague concepts of freedom and equality that fail to specify the sources and consequences of human dignity in a definite way. This jars with an American context that has been powerfully shaped by a very definite, concrete conviction about what freedom and equality mean in political society. They mean freedom from enslavement, equal humanity, impartial rule of law, and equal political rights. These meanings leaped out first from the American colonists' struggle against Great Britain, and then even more clearly and powerfully from the American struggle with race-based slavery. The crucial gains of the abolition and African American civil rights movements in inspiring attachment to and understanding of the American conviction have in large measure been obscured by their recent affiliation with other social justice movements. The progress of communal appreciation for the American conviction and the moral principles that have inspired American political development from the beginning has been progressively replaced by renewed discord and disillusionment. What does conviction mean if it does not change attitudes and behaviors toward African Americans?

There are many and complex reasons for the dysfunction of our current political situation in the United States. This dysfunction doesn't have any single, simple solution. One of the motivating convictions of the Race and the American Story project, though, is that renewed attention to America's defining drama of the struggle for racial justice—the original sin of enslavement and the prospect of ultimate redemption through reconciliation—will inspire a common ground of thought and conviction that can help us out of our political polarization and dysfunction. There is a fundamental confusion in American political thought and discourse today about where we stand and what we should do. A return to where we started, or a point to which we can all return, is in order now more than ever.

Microcosms of this dynamic of polarization and dysfunction are evident at colleges and universities across the country, where the trajectory of political liberalism and academic postmodernism has rapidly outpaced the possibility for mutual learning and dialogue between faculty and students on either side of the divide. At Adam's university, Arizona State, the African and African American Studies program was merged with the Women and Gender Studies program and other programs focusing on social justice and marginalized identities in 2009. It is now the School of Social Transformation. Adam's academic unit at the university, the School of Civic and Economic Thought and Leadership, was created by the state legislature partially in response to this development and related ones on the ASU campus. Some on campus and in the community view this department as "The School of Social Conservatism," a crude misapprehension of what actually goes on in their academic programs, but—as with most crude misapprehensions—not without a grain of truth. Many of the faculty in Social Transformation see their work as opposed to that of the faculty in Civic and Economic Thought and Leadership, and vice versa.

What this shows, among other things, is that social transformation is viewed as opposed to civic education in the United States. Civic education is about political stability, and social transformation is about political disruption. Civic education is about conserving the nation and growing patriots to defend the status quo; social transformation is about wiping out national injustices and growing activists to upset the status quo. There are the defenders of the faith, and there are heretics.

Stephanie's example and perspective completely explode this false dichotomy. As an immigrant to the United States from Africa, with first-generation African American children, and as a lifelong student of and expert on American culture, she has formed a uniquely illuminating perspective on the relationship between American civic education and the imperative for American social transformation. The ongoing experiences of anti-Black racism in the United States are very real and disturbing. Far too many Black Americans suffer the effects of this racism, and far too many white Americans still just don't get it. In Stephanie's view, though, "getting it" includes achieving a deep understanding of American history and the principles of American governance that have contributed to real progress on racial justice through American history. Social transformation is needed in the United States; and this social transformation should be guided in part by the very principles valued by American conservatives—values of freedom, equality, and human dignity.

In the American story, there has been one chapter that both proponents of social transformation and proponents of civic education have been able to return to and reread in unison. This is the chapter dealing with African American rights movements of the nineteenth and twentieth centuries. Rereading this chapter is an education in both citizenship and activism, and an exercise in the true American faith that sometimes looks like heresy. We have begun building bridges between the School of Social Transformation and the School of Civic and Economic Thought and Leadership at ASU—bridges parallel in important ways to those that join contributors to the Race and the American Story project—, and the blueprint for these bridges can be replicated across American society. Adam's School prides itself on fostering civil discourse even in disagreement. This requires a solid common ground to stand on; a place to meet, grapple, and depart as friends. The School of Social Transformation prides itself on fostering attentiveness to social injustice. These two missions meet squarely on issues of racial justice and equality. We may disagree strongly on questions of reparations, the "1619 Project," the causes of the racial wealth gap, or the uniqueness of American slavery; but we agree on the wrongness of enslavement, of lynching, of unequal protection of the law, and of political inequality. And we all agree that these wrongs have historically been perpetrated in a systematic way against Black Americans.

There are important similarities, overlaps, and intersections between African American history and the histories of other marginalized identities in the United States such as American Indians, women, immigrants, Latinos, Chinese, Catholics, Japanese, Irish, LGBTQ people, and others. Systematic, state-sponsored violations of human dignity have occurred in nearly every human society in history, and the United States is no exception to this grim rule. The American conviction about human dignity in particular, though, has grown up alongside and in stark relief against African American history. It owes the greater part of its continuing force to the momentum gained in its struggle against race-based slavery. As racial justice has become conjoined in the popular mind with other social justice causes, the American conviction has receded along with understanding of African American history and rights struggles. Our own conviction is that we will only recover either if we try to recover both.

And if we recover both, the prospects for healing American political dysfunction and polarization will be much improved. What we are missing in American political discourse today is not agreement, consensus, shared vision, cultural homogeneity, a spirit of compromise, or mere civility in the sense of politeness. We can certainly use dashes of these from time to time, like seasoning on food, but they are not the substance of what we are missing. What we are really missing is common ground: shared starting points for thought, discussion, and action. Common ground produces a kind of friendship—a lasting feeling that "we are in this together," no matter our periodic disagreements and conflicts. And racial reconciliation between Black and white in the United States is the perfect—and, though not the only, an absolutely necessary—laboratory, warehouse, and tool shed to build this common ground in America today.

What is this common ground and what does it require? Two things: (1) conceptual agreement on basic moral principles, and (2) a disposition of caring, love, or empathy for other human beings, and particularly other members of one's communities. What these two ingredients do is ensure that all disagreements and conflicts occur within the context of a basic but profound friendship. If you lead with love, everything that follows is transformed. And if you agree on common starting points, common goals become achievable.

Why are African American history and Black–white relations uniquely suited to building this common ground? The first ingredient of agreement on moral principles comes from the relationship between the American conviction about human dignity and African American history. We have argued that this relationship is not only mutually reinforcing but mutually constitutive—you just can't have white American attachment to Founding principles and American greatness or exceptionalism without Black American contributions and rights movements. If there is one thing that binds white America and Black America, it is the same glue that binds American identity as a whole. And that glue is common moral principle, or the American conviction. White and Black Americans—that is, Americans situated socially, legally, and politically as "white" or "Black" as these have been honed and developed since, say, 1619—have been the two identity groups in the United States that have jointly contributed the essentials and the vast majority of elaborations on the American conviction throughout American history. Thomas Jefferson and Prince Hall, Reverend Simeon Jocelyn and John Quincy Adams, Frederick Douglass and Abraham Lincoln, Justice John Marshall Harlan and W. E. B. Du Bois, and numerous other Black and white Americans have been responsible for the chain that has been constructed from the "ringbolt" of the American conviction since its most famous enunciation in the Declaration of Independence.

The second ingredient of the common ground we are searching for— a disposition of love—also resonates in a unique and striking way with African American history. It resonates first and foremost in the sense of stark contrast and tragic absence. For much of American history and in most American communities from the earliest European settlements in North America to today, Black and white Americans have lived side by side but in relations characterized by violence and a continual state of war. These two groups have jointly formed American communities—and the American political community as a whole—in the near total absence of the kind of loving dispositions that are necessary for true common ground. Even when they haven't been diametrically opposed to one another through enslavement or lynching, Black and white American

communities have been separated by legal segregation and social isola-
tion. Adam's own story of growing up in Napa illustrates this. To him,
through no fault of his child self, Black Americans were like foreigners—
existing out there somewhere, but certainly not bound to him by ties of
love or standing beside him on common ground.

Overcoming this tragic absence of the second crucial ingredient of
common ground among Black and white Americans throughout our joint
history would be a monumental achievement. It would upend centuries
of American embarrassment and failure, and make the United States a
shining example for the world. No matter what white Americans may say
about how many Black friends they have, or how vociferously they would
resist the implication that they lack a loving disposition toward Black
Americans, it is obvious in countless small ways and a few large ones that
this is in fact the case. Most of the time there is not any animosity, conscious feeling of superiority, individual discrimination, or violence. There
is an absence rather than a presence—an absence of caring or love.

It is easy to care about people who look like oneself. According to evolu-
tionary biologists, this is one of the reasons children tend to look like their
parents, and particularly their father. Looking alike promotes common
identity among us human animals. But as humans we should know that
we are both animals and something more. As Americans we should know
that, as Frederick Douglass says, we have the potential to make the United
States "the most perfect national illustration of the unity and dignity of the
human family that the world has ever seen."[26] Despite what our animalistic
"moral" feelings might tell us, we know rationally that this unity and dignity of the human family is a reality. Humans are humans, and all humans
are equal in human dignity. And despite our history of inequality, we know
that the United States has been built from the beginning by Black, white,
and brown hands. If we can be smart enough and patriotic enough, we can
summon the disposition of love required to find this second ingredient of
common ground between Black and white Americans.

We cannot say enough about the catalysts of love and empathy to
help us reach our goal of racial justice. After the student movement in
2015, Stephanie found herself answering questions from neighbors who

did not understand what had happened, nor what the students had been protesting about. One well-meaning neighbor said she did not understand why students were talking about racism because "didn't slavery end in the 19th century?" This question shocked Stephanie. All these years living next to these neighbors, breaking bread with them, and they had never understood what her daily life was like as a Black woman. Stephanie gently tried to explain what it was like to be Black in Columbia, Missouri, but the bewildered neighbor remained unmoved. Stephanie's frustration was not that she had to retell stories of trauma, but that the neighbor did not believe these stories. So Stephanie came up with a metaphor to explain empathy to the neighbor. What if white people had to do without sunscreen in the hot sun? This is something Stephanie had never had to apply to her skin. Having grown up close to the Equator with no sunscreen it was not something she had ever used, and her skin did not burn. Stephanie asked her neighbor what would happen if she did not sunscreen? The neighbor replied that her skin would burn, and that it would peel and be painful. Stephanie listened attentively and then responded, "I believe you." She went on to explain that having nonmelanated skin was not her experience but she would not assume to know what the neighbor's life was like. She would simply believe that she was in danger of being hurt simply because of her white skin. This became a great way of explaining empathy and resulted in a TedX talk Stephanie was invited to do in Kansas City. She titled it "SPF/WTF."[27] Like any other analogy, sunburn is not a perfect metaphor for racism because the dangers of living in dark skin cannot be mitigated simply by a trip to the Walgreens aisle to buy some sunscreen product. But it does push those who remain ignorant to the truth of society. If we can achieve true empathy, we can move toward reconciliation.

Once we have achieved this racial reconciliation and its common ground, we will start finding common ground with many other Americans in many other contexts. The American conviction is a powerful force, and the kind of moral agreement this conviction entails would serve as a constant counterweight to our political disagreements, keeping them in proportion and balance. We would have a touchstone that we could all return to when disagreements begin spiraling out of control, instead of forging onward and outward blindly to our own private destinations. We would have something that unifies us with other political and social movements throughout American history, going all the way back to colonial times.

We would also have a deeper appreciation of what it means to be an American, and a stronger sense of common identity with other Americans who might look very different from ourselves. The glue that binds white America and Black America is the glue that binds American identity in general, and it is a glue that inevitably takes us beyond our more particular personal identity and attaches us to the humanity in each other. As vague as this may sound, it is powerful and stable; more powerful and stable, I would argue, than the apparently more concrete and superficially more compelling attachment of "blood and soil."

It has been the consistent loss of this glue, this common ground of conviction and disposition, that has led to the polarization and dysfunction of American political society in recent decades. We have forgotten what it means to be an American, and so we have instead sought our political identities in being Republican or Democrat, conservative or liberal, white, Black, brown, gay, straight, and so on. It is not the presence of these particular identities that is the problem; it is the absence of a substantial American identity that is capable of encompassing all of them. In this case as in others we've come across, we tend to look for the root of our problems in what we see, rather than in what we don't see. And in this case as in so many others, we will begin to solve our problems not by tearing down, but by building up.

LEADING WITH LOVE

For most of American history, the causes of marginalized or oppressed groups have been defined in terms of reduction or destruction: the abolition of slavery, the defeat of segregation, the elimination of discrimination, etc. We need less of the bad things that hold up the progress of freedom, equality and justice. We believe, though, that we have reached a clear moment in our history when what we most urgently need is not less but more. Not just less white privilege, or less institutional racism, or less discrimination, but more charity or love.

The privilege, racism, and discrimination that continue to thrive today are certainly real; and they are in many cases as brutal and overt as they have been at other times in the American past. The fact that they are no longer sanctioned explicitly by the law is a significant point of progress. This outlaw status has not, though, eliminated their operation or even, as Lincoln would say, put them "on course of ultimate extinction." Like imprisoned mafia bosses, they have simply continued their insidious work from beyond the bars of legality—in some ways more effectively and harmfully than they ever did before.

But trying to convince an average white American that privilege, racism, and discrimination are pervasive in modern American society is like trying to convince a detective that an imprisoned convict is responsible for a murder in your neighborhood. What do you mean racism is embedded in American society? Don't you know we abolished slavery and passed the Civil Rights Act? Racism has an alibi just like the suspect in prison. It couldn't be me—I've been illegal for decades!

The fact is that we won't have less of the phenomena referred to as white privilege or institutional racism until we have more charity. Bad or evil things aren't actually things—they are just the absences of good things. Ignorance, for example, isn't something that someone actually *has*—it's simply the absence of knowledge. Hate, similarly, isn't a substantial quality—it's simply the absence of love. Just as the only thing that can reduce ignorance is knowledge, the only thing that can crowd out hate is love.

Looked at this way, trying to fight against privilege, racism, or discrimination without trying to increase charity is like trying to fight ignorance without trying to impart knowledge. This was perhaps the most important insight of Martin Luther King Jr. in designing his strategy of nonviolent resistance or civil disobedience. In his 1958 essay on this topic, King explained how and why "the philosophy of love" was at the very center of the movement he was leading. He explained this in terms of the three distinct words that the ancient Greeks used to name what we call "love": *eros*, *philia*, and *agape*. The one King put at the center of his movement was *agape*, and he defined it this way:

> *Agape* is understanding, creative, redemptive good will for all men. Biblical theologians would say it is the love of God working in the minds of men. It is an overflowing love which seeks nothing in return. And when you come to love on this level you begin to love men not because they are likeable, not because they do things that attract us, but because God loves them and here we love the person who does the evil deed while hating the deed that the person does.[28]

King understood that an equal and just society couldn't be fashioned out of people who merely refrained from doing unjust and unfair things to one another. "Live and let live" has an expiration date set by self-interest, which is precisely the moment at which justice and equality become most important to achieve. Fighting fire with fire—fighting the negativity of racism and unjust discrimination with the negativity of condemnation and destruction—simply doesn't work in a deep or sustainable way.

People need reasons *to* respect other human beings, and not just reasons to not disrespect them. Charity or love needs to actively fill the void of neglect and hatred. Until this happens—first on an individual level and then on the level of society—the void remains, whether or not it shows itself openly.

For many Americans who have grown up and around some form of Christianity, King's religious prescription is the most effective one. Charity is an outgrowth of direct human-to-human connection. If anything else intervenes—race, gender, personality, looks, wealth, status, personal relationship—the connection is lost. Charity can only be sustained as long as one's humanity is in direct contact with another's humanity. It is extremely difficult to achieve and extraordinarily fragile. It requires a state of mind that is completely alien to the outlook of ordinary human life. We are accustomed by the needs and desires of human life to see other people as instrumental in various ways; instrumental to our economic needs, our social needs, our pleasure, or our happiness however we define it. But one's humanity is in no way useful or practically interesting to anyone else's humanity; it is just there to be either noticed or ignored.

Left to our own devices, it is almost inconceivable that any of us would be motivated to linger long in contact with another's humanity. It is, simply, useless. Dwelling on another's humanity only serves to get in the way of our pursuit of benefit and enjoyment through our interaction with them. Another's humanity usually seems like the line at an entrance to a theme park—the drab antechamber to a wonderland of enjoyment, excitement, benefit, and pleasure.

This is why King turned to religion in his elaboration of what was required to transform people and society. Only religion is capable of the kind of extreme perspective shift necessary to incentivize waiting around in line when the roller coasters await. Religion convinces people that they really want to do what they don't want to do, they really want to feel what they don't feel, and that people they encounter really aren't what they seem. Religion can convince people to, in King's words, "love the person who does the evil deed," even when that evil deed might consist in beating, insulting, or cruelly ostracizing oneself.

The religious perspective tells people to see all human beings as children of God, as a part of Creation in common relationship with a Creator. We are all in the same boat; as Frances Harper put it, "we are all bound up together." For those who believe in biblical Revelation, the point is intensified. According to the book of Genesis, human beings are created "in the image and likeness of God." We are not only all like each other, but we are all also like God. For Christians like King the point is stretched even further. Not only are we all part of Creation in common relationship to a Creator, and not only are we all like God Himself as human beings, but the Creator actually became a human being and calls us to union with Him.

The religious perspective embraced by Martin Luther King Jr., the perspective that calls for genuine self-transformation and sacrifice in dedicating oneself to achieving the good for others and for society, differs drastically from the kind of religious perspective that only seeks to justify and excuse existing practices. Religion can be used by human beings to attain selfish ends. It can be used in self-serving ways to justify oppression and injustice. But genuine religion inspires conversion and transformation. Authentic Christianity challenges believers, as King challenged his followers, to really see the face of God in every human being one encounters—even one's enemies. When this happens, the love one feels for other human beings crowds out racism, discrimination, segregation, and injustice. It's not so much that these evils have been defeated or eradicated; it's simply that there's no room for them anymore. Light doesn't destroy darkness; it simply replaces it. John Newton experienced something like this when he was inspired to write the lyrics for "Amazing Grace." His blindness was replaced by a new vision. Defeating evil is good; but evil is only truly defeated when it is replaced by goodness. Only love can defeat hate.

PARALLEL REALITIES

One thing genuine religion does is open up a new perspective on life. It suggests the possibility that there is an entire reality parallel to the mundane, physical one that we normally experience. It provides a reference point for our perception of the world that is actually external to it. It invites us to see the same things we saw before in an entirely different way; to infuse our physical sense of sight with a second sight that is nonphysical, or spiritual.

Dogs have a simple, entirely objective view of the world—food, water, soft places to lie down are what they are, and all dogs respond to them in the same way. As humans we know that a good part of our world is made up by our perceptions of it. These perceptions may be true or false, or they may also be just different. If I say that someone I see has long hair, and you say the same person has short hair, one of us might be wrong—or maybe it's a mullet.

There are piles of great books and movies that are built on this very premise—*The Matrix*, for example. At times we know and are intrigued by the radical possibility that the world is actually very different from what we think we see in front of us, and at other times we cling to our perception of the world with blind tenacity. The latter is the more common disposition, and this is usually for the best. It is better to know a part of reality well than to be confused about all of it; to see clearly from one angle than to not see at all. As humans we rely on intellectual knowledge the way dogs rely on smell, and we have to trust this knowledge implicitly in order to function in our day-to-day lives.

This reliance on what we already know—or what we have to think we know to function comfortably in the world—needs, though, to be balanced by a humble skepticism about our opinions. On the one hand, we need to rely on our understanding of the world to live as humans within it; on the other hand, we need to be aware of the fact that our understanding of the world is necessarily limited, and sometimes flat out wrong. Socrates's life mission was to inspire such humble skepticism in his fellow Athenians. Knowledge of ignorance, according to Socrates, was the prerequisite for a life worth living. Spending his life in constant conversation with others, Socrates witnessed to a truth that we can pursue together but never possess alone.

Probably the best known Socratic story is the "allegory of the cave" from Plato's *Republic*. In this story, prisoners are chained facing a stone wall at the back of a cave. Behind them, at the cave's opening, are objects being carried by people who are walking back and forth. The prisoners can see the shadows of the objects on the cave wall, but they are unable to see the objects themselves or the people carrying them. The prisoners have, in fact, never in their lives been able to turn their heads around to see the sources of the shadows with which they are familiar. After setting this scene, one of Socrates's friends comments on the strangeness of the situation. What is Socrates getting at in setting up this convoluted scenario? Who are these prisoners supposed to represent? Socrates's response: "They are like us."

Jesus of Nazareth provides a similar lesson. A constant refrain in his teaching is to see through the visible, material, conventional reality in front of us to a higher and very different reality beyond. "My kingdom is not of this world" could be the subtitle of the Gospels. The Pharisees look great on the outside, but they are rotten within. The widow looks poor when she drops her penny in the box, but she gave more than anyone else. Rich people seem to have it great, but it's the poor beggar Lazarus who ends up on top. "The first shall be last, and the last shall be first." Jesus, who claims to be the most powerful king in the world, is ignominiously crucified alongside criminals. To one of them, in the most extreme example of this contrast between what seems and what really is, Jesus says—while both of them are hanging painfully on crosses, torturously inching toward death—"this day you will be with me in paradise."

This theme of attempting to see a parallel reality was a key cornerstone of Martin Luther King Jr.'s strategy of nonviolent civil disobedience. Citing both Socrates and Jesus frequently as inspiration, and building on the resonances of their teachings in the example of Gandhi, King's success was built largely on his ability to convince others that the physical, visible reality around them didn't matter. It didn't matter because there was a parallel reality behind and beyond it that was much more powerful and lasting. In the last speech of his life, delivered the day before he was assassinated, King made this point as directly as Socrates and Jesus ever did. Speaking of Bull Connor's infamous command to turn the fire hoses on civil rights activists, King said, "He knew a kind of physics that somehow didn't relate to the transphysics that we knew about. And that was the fact that there was a certain kind of fire that no water could put out."[29] Bull Connor really did know one part of reality—the physical part about the force of shooting water and its effect on human bodies—but he was entirely ignorant of another part of reality: the "transphysical" part about the force of love and its effect on human souls. King's point is that Bull Connor wasn't actually wrong; his knowledge was just too narrow and limited. "He knew" something, he saw part of the world accurately, he just wasn't aware of the part that King and his fellow activists were in touch with.

King knew that finding common ground on issues of racial justice in American society was more a matter of learning than unlearning, of opening eyes rather than shutting them. Opposing racism—being an "antiracist," as Ibram Kendi would say—is good, but encountering humanity with a wide embrace is better. Like Aristotle's reflections on justice and friendship, the latter includes and transcends the former. Leading with love, and listening with respect, opens up a parallel reality that complements and transforms the one with which we are familiar.

This is the experience we have had in teaching and learning about race in American society with each other and with our colleagues, students, and friends. During recent events we have hosted in the Race and the American Story project, we have been joined by family members of our presenters and faculty. These are people who, though wonderful and delightful in many ways, may not have ever encountered or thought about the topics we were discussing. Sometimes this initial encounter may feel uncomfortable or even shocking—like the feeling of jumping into a cold pool on a hot day. Seeing a new perspective is not like hearing a new argument; it is immersive and disorienting. In this situation it is tempting to jump right back out, dry off, and go back inside to the comfort of one's own living room. One goal of the Race and the American Story project is to continue to invite people to try out a new perspective, to jump back in, and to let go of their preconceptions and prejudices. Our hope is that, after jumping in a few times, people might begin to say to themselves: I could get used to this!

Freedom and Hope, Liberation and Love

TOWARD A NEW AMERICAN STORY

American history can be a boring subject—a collection of facts, events, people, and (worst of all) dates from a past that is dead and gone. History buffs are usually not the life of the party. What does it matter that American Independence was actually declared by the Continental Congress on July 2 rather than July 4? Do I need to know that both Abraham Lincoln and Charles Darwin were born on February 12, 1809? Unless I want to get onto *Jeopardy* or win at Trivial Pursuit, the answer seems to be a resounding "not much" and "no."

This is the way most of us have learned our national history; and this is why not many of us know or care about it. In recent years, though, histories of a different sort have gained a hearing.[1] These histories have uncovered new stories embedded within the stale narratives we were all taught as children. Stories of groups of people most Americans knew nothing about because they existed on the margins of our long-standing national narratives; stories of individuals—some familiar and some previously unknown—that shed entirely new light on times, places, and people we thought we knew.

Many of these newer histories have disrupted the stale and ossified American narrative. They have made American history come alive again.

Race and the American Story. Stephanie Shonekan and Adam Seagrave, Oxford University Press.
© Oxford University Press 2024. DOI: 10.1093/oso/9780197767689.003.0006

Sometimes, though, this work has been like bringing a corpse to the dinner table; interesting, perhaps, but distinctly unwelcome to people just trying to enjoy a good meal. These newer histories about marginalized and forgotten people who have played crucial roles in the progress of American society have sometimes upset the triumphalist American narrative many white Americans grew up with. They have been faced with the challenge of not only learning new things, but of relearning things they thought they already knew, and even of potentially getting rid of opinions about the past that they really enjoyed having.

The study of American history has become less about events and dates and more about people and their stories. It has become less about the checkpoints or rest stops and more about stopping to smell the flowers—or, sometimes, the skunks—along the way. This is a good thing, at least as a complement to the traditional names-and-dates approach to American history. It has also, however, led to a significant problem. We used to have a simple, unified approach to understanding and interpreting American history. Now, with the proliferation of individual and particular group stories that have complicated relationships with the traditionally mainstream ones, we have lost this simple unity. Having eaten of the tree of historical knowledge, we are now confused.

It is the belief of the authors of this book, however, that we can recover a unified approach to the American story. It will not be as simple as it used to be, but it will be stronger and more beautiful for its diversity. We have told our individual stories in order to illustrate this important truth. We have had vastly different life paths, with very different cultural backgrounds and upbringings. Each of our personal stories has intersected with the American story at different points and from different directions, giving us different perspectives on American identity and history.[2] We have different religious beliefs and different political opinions. We look different from one another. And yet each of our stories fits equally within the American story.

Our stories are just two out of millions, but they show how the American story can truly be one of humanity as it has always aspired to be. In this concluding chapter, we will make a beginning toward telling this story in two ways: first, in the form of historical narrative; and second, in the form of musical narrative. These two ways of weaving an American story intersect with each other at the waypoints of freedom and hope, liberation and love. They also plainly display the outward-facing character of the American story. The American story has always been built through a distinctive combination of native and foreign materials; and it has always claimed an audience extending far beyond its own shores.

Frederick Douglass once said that the United States has a mission to be "the most perfect national illustration of the unity and dignity of the human family that the world has ever seen."[3] We all know that the American story has fallen tragically short of this ideal—so tragically short, in fact, that many now doubt that this ever was a part of our national story at all. American ideals of humanity seem to many like a smokescreen shrouding American history in a pleasant lie that serves only to uphold and excuse systemic injustice. Even if this has often been true, we have the materials to build the American story anew on the foundation of humanity and freedom. An honest and inspiring American story that can unify all Americans is out there, waiting to be told, played, and sung.

TWO AMERICAN HISTORICAL NARRATIVES

Telling that new story has to begin by gleaning what we can from the old ones. What we have now are two broad narratives about our American past that largely contradict one another. Each disrupts and counteracts the other, essentially forcing Americans to choose between them. These competing American stories have recently become tightly wound together with competing American political ideologies and parties. Political party identification and conservative/progressive alignment has reinforced the divisions between Americans who endorse these different historical narratives.

One American historical narrative can be called the Mount Rushmore version—MR for short. This narrative begins with the events, people, and documents of 1776. Washington and Jefferson serve as its twin pillars.

MR holds George Washington up as the consummate hero and symbol of American virtue. He embodies the unity of purpose, determination, and perseverance that characterized the Revolutionary struggle against the tyranny of Great Britain. Washington was the only person who could have kept the American Union together through the course of the war, and he was the only person who could have ensured its successful transition out of it in the 1780s. With all of the power in his hands at the end of the Revolutionary War, he gave it up willingly to become a private citizen and allow for the preservation of the freedom and equality for which he had fought. When the Constitutional Convention of 1787 was in dire need of legitimacy, Washington agreed to preside over the proceedings. When he could have continued in office as president indefinitely, he chose to retire from political life and allow for the first peaceful transition of national executive authority. Upon his death, he provided for the emancipation of nearly all of his slaves.

There is nothing like a bloody conflict against a tyrannical king to kick off a national narrative. Washington's exploits as a military leader throughout this conflict are legendary. His daring crossing of the freezing Delaware River on Christmas night 1776 to turn the early tide of the war inspired famous poetry and paintings. It is difficult to find record of anyone at the time who didn't think Washington was the bee's knees. Washington speaks to the emotional, ra-ra patriot in all of us. He gives flag-wavers across the country everything they could want in a national hero.

The other hero of 1776 for MR is Thomas Jefferson. Jefferson is the father of the "American mind." As author of the Declaration of Independence, Jefferson gave voice to the ideals of world-historical significance on which our national independence was first established. Jefferson's pen was the fitting complement to Washington's sword. No one but Jefferson could have stated our fundamental American political principles with such clarity and eloquence. The words "all men are created equal" reverberate throughout American history like a beloved refrain that inspires each generation anew.

Jefferson is the perfect counterpart to Washington for the more intellectually inclined. He was also there on ground-zero at the most crucial moment of the Revolutionary War. He had read people like Locke and Bacon, and was a crucial figure in the flowering of intellectual achievement that is now known as the Enlightenment. In addition to his authorship of the brilliant Declaration of Independence and other well-known writings, Jefferson founded the first public university in the United States, the University of Virginia. He is thus a kind of patron saint for many academics and scholars who find a place within MR. Jefferson shows that America is not only about the outpouring of righteous violence on the battlefield, but also about truth and right. America has a sensitive side too.

Jefferson and Washington as twin hero-pillars of MR corresponds also with the Declaration of Independence and the Constitution as twin document-pillars of this narrative. MR interprets the Declaration of Independence as an enduring and true account of political principles.[4] These principles both justified American independence and the war establishing it, and also signaled the beginning of American exceptionalism and world leadership through their universal applicability. When the Declaration said "all men are created equal," it meant "all human beings are created equal." The Declaration was aspirational in its intent, and has been inspirational in its effect. MR holds the Declaration of Independence to be the greatest statement of human liberty in history.

The Constitution, according to MR, built the superstructure of American institutions squarely on the foundation of the true and enduring principles found in the Declaration. The Preamble of the Constitution announces this by beginning with the ringing words "We the People," and the rest of the document continues this liberating message in various ways. As Frederick Douglass said in his 5th of July speech in 1852—something believers in MR love to note—the Constitution is "a glorious liberty document." The Constitution packaged the glorious moment of American Founding into something that could continue to guide American political life in perpetuity. As the oldest written constitution in the world, it provides an enduring symbol of America's exceptional greatness. It is a testament to the wisdom of the Founding generation. The Constitution allowed the principles of the Revolution to outlive the war itself, and provide the "blessings of liberty" to future American generations.

Subscribers to the MR narrative, especially in recent years, acknowledge the imperfections in the people and documents of the Founding Era. They openly regret the fact that people like Washington and Jefferson were unable to abolish the evil of racial slavery during their lifetimes.[5] They readily admit that the institution of slavery was an unfortunate blot on the otherwise remarkable and positive achievements of the Founders. They also regret the unjust treatment of American Indian nations, who were alternately slaughtered and displaced from their land throughout the course of early American history.

But this is right where Abraham Lincoln comes in and saves the day. Through his leadership in the Civil War and his eloquent reaffirmation and reinterpretation of the principles of the Declaration of Independence, Lincoln became Washington and Jefferson rolled into one. Lincoln shows how one can celebrate the achievements of the American Founders while admitting their shortcomings. Lincoln provided a powerful interpretation of the Founding Era documents that absolved them of implication in the evils of their time, and even recast them as actively opposed to these evils. Slavery was treated by the leading Founders as a "necessary evil"; something they wanted to get rid of but couldn't. The Declaration of Independence said "all men are created equal" with an eye to inspiring the future generations who would have the ability to apply this ideal in practice. The majority of the Constitution-writers were opposed to slavery, and wanted to "put it on course of ultimate extinction." The Declaration of Independence is at the heart of the Constitution like the Proverbial "golden apple" within a "picture of silver."

Lincoln's refounding is a necessary complement to the original founding, according to MR. It showed, crucially, that the power of American ideals and the American political tradition was great enough to overcome even the evil of the institution of slavery. With the Emancipation Proclamation and the 13th Amendment, Lincoln led the next great step of the triumphal march of American history toward the ever more perfect achievement of liberty and equality.

Lincoln's relationship with the formerly enslaved African American Frederick Douglass is of crucial importance for MR's self-understanding as an American historical narrative.[6] Initially critical of Lincoln for his refusal to embrace the cause of abolition throughout his early political career and much of his presidency, Douglass comes to appreciate Lincoln's political prudence in achieving what he could for the cause of liberty and equality. This appreciation was expressed most clearly in Douglass's oration in memory of Lincoln given at the unveiling of the Freedmen's Monument in 1876. This is an additional reason why conservatives have rushed to the defense of the Freedmen's Monument in response to recent calls for its removal. Not only is this monument a symbol of Lincoln's achievements; it is a symbol of Frederick Douglass's blessing of Lincoln and his crucial role within the MR narrative.

In addition to his positive relationship with Lincoln, Frederick Douglass plays an important role in the MR version of American history in his own right. If Washington embodied the Revolutionary struggle against the tyranny of Britain, Douglass embodied the abolitionist's struggle against the evil of slavery. Like Washington and Jefferson, Douglass was an extraordinary individual. More than anyone else in American history, Douglass exemplified what it means to "pull yourself up from your bootstraps." Escaping from slavery as a teenager, and having taught himself how to read and write, Douglass went on to become one of the most successful and influential orators in American history.

Initially agreeing with fellow abolitionist William Lloyd Garrison that the US Constitution was a proslavery document and therefore fit only for the flames, Douglass made a dramatic conversion to see the Constitution as fundamentally opposed to slavery. In one of his most famous speeches, delivered on the 5th of July 1852, Douglass referred to the American Founders as "truly great men." The Declaration of Independence contained "saving principles." The Constitution was "a glorious liberty document." Although Douglass didn't pull his punches when it came to the need to condemn and abolish slavery and, later, the oppressions of lynching and segregation, he grounded his opposition to racial injustice on the same principles of natural human rights that had guided the American Founding.

The example of Frederick Douglass is so powerful and important for MR because of his ability to personally overcome enslavement and embrace a positive and inspirational account of American history.[7] Lincoln's leadership in the Civil War overcame and redeemed the shortcomings of an otherwise exceptionally true and good American Founding. The single conspicuous crack in the foundation had been patched up once and for all. In his Second Inaugural Address, Lincoln puts this in terms of Divine Providence exacting the precise amount of suffering from the war necessary to counterbalance the suffering from the evil of slavery. Lincoln, however, was not someone who had personally suffered the consequences of this evil. He couldn't speak for the formerly enslaved and their descendants. Could they see it the same way? Frederick Douglass did, and his example has become a crucial piece of evidence supporting the MR version of American history. If Frederick Douglass could escape slavery and then come to embrace Lincoln and American Founding principles, all formerly enslaved African Americans could. The single most troubling exclusion from the universalism of Jefferson's Declaration and the democratic republicanism of the Constitution can confidently be erased.

The next major checkpoint for the MR narrative comes with the Martin Luther King Jr.–led civil rights movement. The intervening 100 years since Lincoln's assassination were quiet in terms of major progress in the march of American history toward more perfect realization of our Founding aspirations. The women's suffrage movement of the early twentieth century is the exception, though this is often muted as an achievement due to its association with the later waves of feminism that would usher in *Roe v. Wade*, the sexual revolution, and the challenging of traditional gender roles.

Martin Luther King Jr. arrives in the mid-twentieth century as an anachronistic resurrection of Frederick Douglass. His "I Have a Dream" speech, delivered on the steps of the Lincoln Memorial 100 years after the Emancipation Proclamation, reaffirmed the aspirational quality of American Founding principles just as Frederick Douglass's 5th of July speech had. In this speech in particular, King placed the cause of African American civil rights firmly on MR's familiar ground: American history as the progress of true ideals that would lead to ever greater achievement of liberty and justice for all. As Douglass had said, the problem was not with the foundation of the Declaration and Constitution but with the "moral blindness" of individual people who couldn't see how these documents should be applied in practice. With this obstruction removed, the "saving principles" contained in these documents could continue to spread their salutary influence. In King's famous metaphor, the "promissory note" itself had always been good; the problem had always been mismanagement of funds by misguided individuals. With the proper funds in place, the check was as good as ever.[8]

As with Frederick Douglass, and in contrast to Malcolm X, King provided powerful evidence that even those excluded from the initial application of American principles of liberty and equality could still celebrate these principles and admire their authors. The content and circumstances of the "I Have a Dream" speech were picture-perfect in this respect. King's delivery of the speech on the steps of the Lincoln Memorial paralleled Frederick Douglass's oration in memory of Lincoln at the dedication of the Freedmen's Monument. For those who subscribe to the MR account of American history, both instances are important reminders of the power of American ideals and the inevitability of their progress through history.

The other American historical narrative can be called the Untold Story version—US for short. This version begins with the events and people of 1619. This was the year that the first enslaved Africans arrived in the British North American colonies, inaugurating years and generations of American stories that wouldn't ever find their way into American history books. The history of enslaved African Americans was very closely, even inextricably intertwined with the history of European Americans in the societies that would become the United States. The lives of the people whose faces are carved into Mount Rushmore itself were profoundly, indelibly shaped by their coexistence with African Americans whose faces were forgotten to the MR version of history.[9] To give the best-known example, it was only in the last couple of decades that Thomas Jefferson's intimate relationship with the enslaved Sally Hemings was brought to historical light.

But the African American story, like the individual stories of almost all African Americans over the course of four hundred years, is mostly absent from the MR version of American history. So, too, are the stories of other non-European American peoples who have had very important, but less closely and extensively intertwined, relationships with European American societies in the United States: American Indians, Latinos, and immigrants from Asia, the Middle East, and elsewhere. In addition to these groups of non-European racial, ethnic, and national origin, the stories of American women are mostly absent from the MR version of history. All of these groups or types of people have had profound impacts on American history. Their stories, though, were relegated to the sidelines by the dominant MR account for centuries until they began to be highlighted by the US account.

The US account received its initially most famous articulation in Howard Zinn's 1980 book *A People's History of the United States*. In Zinn's account, the US version of history is provided as a corrective critique of the MR version. The MR version had upheld systems of elite domination and oppression throughout American history; the US version would empower the marginalized and oppressed by giving voice to their previously neglected stories. Celebrated by progressives and reviled by conservatives, Zinn's book remains a widely referenced symbol of the division between the two accounts of American history today.

The more recent successor to Zinn's book in the popular understanding is the *New York Times Magazine*'s "1619 Project." The title and framing of this project were designed by editor Jake Silverstein to sharpen the division between proponents of the MR and US accounts. The MR account vests the number 1776 with an almost sacred symbolism. This comes in large part from the authority of Abraham Lincoln. In the Gettysburg Address, Lincoln had translated the significance of the American Founding into a math problem: "Four score and seven years ago . . . ." Lincoln hereby cast the importance of the events, people, and documents of the American Revolutionary War in concrete numeric terms as a simple four-digit number: 1776. This extreme simplification of the MR account in Lincoln's skillful rhetoric opened the door to the similarly extreme simplification of the US account in the *New York Times Magazine*'s marketing strategy. With the importance of the American Founding having been distilled into a single number, the *New York Times Magazine* could easily signal its alternative account by a single number as well: 1619. As Silverstein explains in the introductory Editor's Note, "The goal of the 1619 Project . . . is to reframe American history by considering what it would mean to regard 1619 as our nation's birth year."

The scope of the US version of American history is immense, and fully coextensive with the MR version. It is not just a collection of vignettes or anecdotes of interest to particular subsets of the American people. It is more than simply a not-so-fun facts version of American history. As Silverstein puts it in the "1619 Project," "Out of slavery—and the anti-Black racism it required—grew nearly everything that has truly made America exceptional." US claims that the oppressive and unjust practices endorsed or perpetuated by early Americans—particularly the practice of African American enslavement—have been so pervasive in American society from the beginning as to be definitive of what the American system represents. Slavery and anti-Black racism aren't, as MR claims, in contradiction with the aspirational ideals of the American Founding. This claim of contradiction elevates the importance of abstract ideals relative to concrete material realities, downplaying the importance of actual injustice and oppression. Abstract ideals like liberty and equality, according to US, grow out of oppressors' need to rationalize and distract from their oppressive practices. The more we focus on these ideals, the less we acknowledge the evil reality in front of us. The US account of American history is the real story; the MR version is a myth.

The US account echoes Indiana Senator John Pettit's famous claim in 1854 that "all men are created equal" was a "self-evident lie." Pettit himself actually disbelieved in human equality. Proponents of the US account believe in human equality but don't believe the signers of the Declaration of Independence, or Jefferson himself, did. Coming out of Jefferson's mouth, "all men are created equal" is false. It is false because it can't be a genuine or authentic statement of what Jefferson or the other signers of the document believed. Though "all men are created equal" might be a truth in the general sense, it could not have been "Jefferson's truth." As Justice Taney said in his *Dred Scott* opinion, "if the language, as understood in that day, would embrace them, the conduct of the distinguished men who framed the Declaration of Independence would have been utterly and flagrantly inconsistent with the principles they asserted. . . . Yet the men who framed this declaration were great men . . . and incapable of asserting principles inconsistent with those on which they were acting."[10] In other words, the practices of slavery and anti-Black racism among the American Founders define the meaning of their abstract ideals. The two are inextricably intertwined.

For the US account, the entirety of the history cherished by the MR version is a false narrative told by the victors. It is a series of myths that don't tell what actually happened but only what supports ongoing social hierarchies based on race, gender, class, and other arbitrary categories. It is not about the past, but about the present and future. It is about rationalizing and explaining away the extensive injustices and violence that were required to erect the institutions and systems that uphold the status quo in the United States today.

This means that uncovering the real, actual historical record also serves the cause of social justice. This connection was on vivid display throughout Malcolm X's speeches. To take one example: the MR version of history has a special place for the Mayflower Compact. Like the Constitutional Convention in 1787, the Mayflower Compact furnishes an inspiring scene of group deliberation and agreement for the common good. The Pilgrims who landed at Plymouth Rock in 1620 were devout Christians who believed in the rule of law, civic friendship, and communal self-government. Malcolm X turns the story of the Mayflower Compact on its head by telling it from the perspective of the enslaved African Americans who arrived at almost exactly the same time in Virginia. Speaking to the descendants of these enslaved African Americans, he says "We didn't land on Plymouth Rock. Plymouth Rock landed on us."

Malcolm X's imagery here is more complex and profound than it seems at first glance. A rock symbolizes a foundation—stable, firm, permanent. Coming from the ocean and landing on a rock signals the transition from mystery and uncertainty to system and order. In retrospect, Plymouth Rock is representative of the American Founding. It is, in fact, like an arch-founding; the founding before the founding. Malcolm X takes this symbol of the American Founding and makes it a symbol of crushing oppression. A rock can stabilize or it can crush, depending on which side of it you're on.

This image of a foundation simultaneously supporting a sprawling superstructure and compacting everything beneath it shows how serious the opposition between the MR and US versions of the American story are. It is not that each version has different heroes; it is that the heroes of the one are the villains of the other. It is not that each version emphasizes different aspects of American history; their emphases are nearly identical, but opposite. The very things that are upheld as admirable by the one are reviled as abominable by the other. The ideals of the Declaration of Independence are cherished by MR as a lodestar of political aspiration and a unifying touchstone. These same ideals are vilified by US as the ideology of a dominant group, a tool used by those in power to maintain it for themselves and to excuse the withholding of it from others.

There is no middle ground or compromise between these two accounts of American history. Each is defined in opposition to the other. And because national narratives are crucial to the articulation of political alternatives in the present, these opposed accounts provide enormous momentum behind our partisan clashes today.[11] Each of our personal stories is influenced by the stories of the communities within which we find ourselves: our families, our friends, our workplaces, our towns, etc. Our national community is in one way the weakest of these because it is the largest and farthest from our direct, concrete experience. In another way, though, it is the strongest. It is more comprehensive than any of these other levels of community, including them all within it. It is a kind of peak of these other communities, enabling them all to survive and thrive under its support and protection. Our national community challenges citizens to lift ourselves up beyond our day-to-day lives to consider the good of others, as well as the common good of an entire community. This appeals to our deep human need to work for the ennobling causes of justice and truth.

National narratives are, in this way, closely aligned with what we call "worldviews." The political community is the most far-reaching and ambitious community of which human beings can be a part. Because of this, our own comprehensive perspectives on the world tend to be reflective in some way of our national narratives; and we in turn often try to project our own comprehensive perspectives onto the palette of our particular national landscape. The political community is the highest, broadest, and longest-lasting arena within which individuals can authentically live out their deepest-held convictions.

The MR account of American history identifies closely with the intellectual and cultural heritage of Western Civilization. Ancient Greek ideas of virtue, Roman ideas of law, Renaissance ideas of republicanism, English ideas of liberty, and Christian religious beliefs all combined in producing the worldviews of most of the leading American Founders. Although they had been transplanted an ocean away, the European American colonists had deep psychological connections with these cultural roots. The MR account celebrates this heritage and views American history as in many ways the peak of Western Civilization.

The US version of American history, on the other hand, is connected to the postmodern worldview that reacts against the hegemony of Western Civilization. Every new or previously neglected story of injustice and oppression provides an argument against the purity of MR's cultural heritage and ideals. Uncovering these stories exposes the hollowness of MR's glittering generalities for what they really are: tools for the maintenance of those in power. Postmodern literary and political theory replaces the idea of objective interpretation or discovery with that of subjective narratives that are unavoidably and pervasively influenced by dynamics of power. There is my truth and there is your truth; there is no Truth. For the US narrative of American history, there are individual and group stories; there is no American story. To the extent that there is an American story, it is not particularly uplifting or unique. It is the story of power dynamics played out in one place that are similar to power dynamics playing out elsewhere around the world.

The gulf between these two versions of American history and between their corresponding world views is massive. The individuals who hold them cannot join together to build a shared, self-governing political society. They can only be forced together by a dictator. There is no possibility

either for a coherent combination of the two, or for a compromise between them that could serve as actionable common ground. The question
of which narrative is truer or more historically accurate, though interesting, is irrelevant to the practical problem of building a shared political
society. Doors 1 and 2 are dead ends, and there is no Door 1½. What does
Door 3 look like?

A NEW HISTORICAL NARRATIVE

Retelling the American story in a more honest, inspiring, and inclusive way
begins, strangely enough, with noticing how misleading the Declaration
of Independence is when it states that "all men are created equal." This
is misleading not because it isn't true—understood correctly, it certainly
is—, but because the concept of equality wasn't of primary importance
to the American colonists at the time. In Jefferson's Declaration, equality
seems primary and rights seem secondary. The self-evident truth that "all
men are created equal" comes before the self-evident truth that "they are
endowed by their Creator with certain unalienable rights." Equality is cast
as the foundation of rights, as the most fundamental value for which the
colonists were fighting the Revolution.

In the context of 1776, though, this description of the central importance of equality comes out of left-field, or at least deep shortstop. Rights
and liberties, not equality, were the watchwords of the day. A quick glance
across the titles of well-known pamphlets, documents, and sermons of the
time clearly reveals this: Jefferson's own "A Summary View of the Rights of
British America," James Otis's "The Rights of the British Colonies Asserted
and Proved," Elisha Williams's "The Essential Rights and Liberties of
Protestants," George Mason's "Virginia Declaration of Rights," the later
"Bill of Rights," and so on. The Declaration itself is not a Declaration of
"Equality," but a Declaration of "Independence." If there were any "Sons
of Equality" in the 1760s and 1770s, they were of little consequence. The
"Sons of Liberty," on the other hand, were essential to the cause of the
Revolution.

The overwhelming sense one gets from reading Revolutionary and Founding Era writings is the importance of rights and liberties—what we more often call "freedom" today. The American colonists didn't want to be taxed without their consent, given laws by a distant, nonrepresentative Parliament, subjected to the arbitrary rule of a king, policed by a foreign military force, or tried for crimes by biased judges. On all of these subjects the colonists produced volumes of petitions, pamphlets, sermons, and articles. In all of these writings they based their claims on rights and liberties, as well as the similar concepts of privileges and immunities. Equality appears in a clearly secondary and supporting role: the colonists argue that they possess the rights, liberties, privileges, and immunities of British subjects or of human beings in equal measure with those in Britain. Saying these early American arguments were about equality would be about as informative as asking a bartender for a drink with equal parts.

The importance of emphasizing freedom rather than equality is clear also from their respective opposites. The opposite of equality is inequality. Inequality can certainly be a bad thing, but it isn't obviously objectionable from a moral standpoint, and wasn't so particularly at the time of the American Revolution. There may be justified inequalities or unjustified inequalities. There may be equality in certain respects and inequality in others. Equality is a mathematical concept adapted in particular cases to take on a moral meaning. Inequality in number is morally neutral; no one objects to the fact that the number two is unequal to the number five. It is only inequality in specific moral categories that becomes a moral problem.

The opposite of freedom is slavery, which is always bad. Freedom is an inherently moral concept, and this makes slavery—as its opposite— an inherently immoral one. Almost no one at the time of the American Revolution would have denied this. Distinctions between justified or unjustified slavery, or slavery in certain respects but not in others, had no meaning then as they wouldn't now. This may seem to conflict with what we know about the institution of slavery throughout the American colonies, and especially widespread in the Southern colonies, at this time. It is true that many American colonists viewed the enslavement of African

Americans as a practical necessity. Many colonists profited greatly—directly and indirectly—from slavery, and were therefore interested in excusing it as unavoidable or as a "necessary evil." But slavery remained for them an evil that called for some excuse or exception. It was not a "positive good" with an independent justification, as it would become for Southern slaveholders decades later.

This becomes particularly clear when one notices how often the American colonists of the Revolutionary Era used the term "slavery" in complaining about their own treatment at the hands of the British. In his "A Summary View of the Rights of British America," written just two years before the Declaration of Independence, Jefferson accuses King George III of committing "a series of oppressions, begun at a distinguished period, and pursued unalterably through every change of ministers, [which] too plainly prove a deliberate and systematical plan of reducing us to slavery."[12] James Otis similarly argued that by having the legislative power of their representative colonial assemblies usurped by the British government, British subjects in the American colonies had been "reduced to a state of slavery, and subject to the despotic rule of others." In support of his case for American colonial freedom, Otis asserted that "A state has no right to make slaves of the conquered."[13]

These are far from isolated examples. The petitions, letters, and pamphlets of the time abound with explicit references to the state of "slavery" into which the American colonists would be reduced if they failed to oust the British. Although the colonists did assert their equality to their fellow subjects in Britain, their complaint was never primarily one of unequal treatment. In fact, when Thomas Whately presented his "virtual representation" argument demonstrating persuasively that the American colonists were treated equally with 9/10 of the subjects in Britain with respect to representation in Parliament, his argument fell completely flat. The American colonists in the 1760s and 1770s didn't care much about being equal to fellow subjects in Britain—they cared about the fact that they were "subjects" at all. They wanted to be free, self-governing citizens. They weren't worried about being second-class citizens; they were worried about being slaves.

"The American mind" was much closer to what George Mason had said in the Virginia Declaration of Rights: "That all men are by nature equally free and independent." Equality was important almost exclusively as an adverb throughout the writings of the time: equally free, equally independent, equally endowed with rights. In the Declaration of Independence, Jefferson and the Continental Congress unilaterally promoted equality from adverbial to nominal status. This sounds harmless enough, and perhaps even commendable. The problem is that, in so doing, they simultaneously demoted freedom.

There might seem to be little difference, to our distorted hindsight, between the Declaration's "all men are created equal" and Mason's "all men are by nature equally free and independent." Upon consideration, though, it becomes clear that much is left out in the Declaration's version. Mason's is like the following statement: "Joe and Jim are similarly eager to begin eating the delicious meal." The Declaration's says this: "Joe and Jim are similar." These statements are obviously not equivalent. There's nothing at all about a delicious meal or eagerness to eat it in the Declaration-style statement. And in the case of the actual Declaration of Independence, what is left out—freedom—is much more significant.

Jefferson's and the Continental Congress's distinctive phrasing choices in the Declaration's second paragraph are often attributed to mellifluousness—the desire to sound pleasing to the ear. The "pursuit of happiness," for example, excites the imagination and roles off the tongue more easily than John Locke's "property." They certainly achieved this goal with "all men are created equal" as well. No phrase has become embedded in American culture more deeply than this one. Jefferson's original draft version, though, had added "and independent:" "all men are created equal and independent." It's not clear from the historical record why this was removed from the final version. What is clear is that this removal makes an enormous difference.

"Independent" may be a synonym for "free," but not for "equal." It is possible that "independent" and "free" were omitted from the Declaration of Independence because of one of their antonyms: enslaved. Equality is, of course, clearly opposed to slavery as well. The antislavery thrust of "all men are created equal" was widely noticed at the time, both within and outside the American states. But as an opposite for slavery, equality falls far short of freedom (and independence is likely somewhere in between). It takes a conscious mental operation, however simple, to go from human equality to the injustice of slavery. This is the mental operation Lincoln walked through in a note to himself in 1854: "If A can prove, however conclusively, that he may, of right, enslave B—why may not B snatch the same argument, and prove equally, that he may enslave A?"[14] This is a simple enough argument, but it is an argument nonetheless. The idea of equality doesn't immediately exclude the idea of slavery as its defined opposite.

In his petition for the abolition of slavery in Massachusetts in 1777, Prince Hall made the more direct argument from slavery's definitional opposite: the "natural and inalienable right to that freedom which the Great Parent of the Universe has bestowed equally on all mankind."[15] Making the clearest argument he could on the basis of the principles of the American Revolution, Hall followed the established practice of emphasizing "freedom" and employing equality in a supporting, adverbial role. A statement by the Continental Congress that "all men are created free"—or "free and equal," as the 1780 Massachusetts Constitution has it—would have made its coexistence with the institution of slavery an immediate definitional contradiction. By retreating from this direct contradiction just far enough—to equality—the Continental Congress paved the way for others to make arguments against slavery without having to actually admit to this conclusion themselves.

The Declaration of Independence's statement that "all men are created equal" is a true statement that has been a powerful force for positive change throughout American history. Without freedom, though, this statement is like a two-legged stool; it is incomplete, unstable, and insufficient for underpinning a unified American story. Freedom is the heart and soul of the American story. Freedom is uniquely human and unavoidably normative; it defines human dignity, demands universal respect, and points to human fulfillment and flourishing. From the beginning, freedom has been interwoven with the fabric of American culture, and it has echoed throughout American history like a mantra or refrain.

The American embrace of freedom is the way in which the American story has claimed an important role in human history. As the nineteenth-century German philosopher Hegel noticed, "The Idea of Freedom" has been in many ways the focal point of human consciousness throughout universal human history. The exercise of freedom and the aspiration for more complete freedom, Hegel plausibly argues, has driven human progress throughout history. There is a reason why Mel Gibson (as William Wallace) yells "FREEEEEEEEEEDOM!" in *Braveheart* rather than "JUSTICE!," "EQUALITY!," or "HAPPINESS!" As noble as these other concepts are, they don't quite match the importance or motivational power of freedom in the human experience.

Since the early seventeenth century, the North American colonies that would become the United States have claimed a particular relationship to freedom. The Puritans and other groups, religious and nonreligious, left Europe for North America in order to obtain greater freedom than was possible for them in Europe. Simultaneous with this culmination of a search for freedom in North America was the beginning of another, even more dramatic one: that of the enslaved Africans who first arrived in Jamestown in 1619. At the exact same time that European North Americans were celebrating the dawn of newfound freedom, African North Americans were entering the long night of slavery.

Freedom was at the center of both of these developments. Whether by its presence or its absence, freedom defined the American story from its beginning.[16] Like a fulcrum, freedom was the single reference point both for the glorious "city upon a hill" enjoyed by European settlers on one side, and the infamous valley of enslavement suffered by African Americans on the other. The enjoyment of freedom has divided white and Black Americans from the beginning, but the desire for freedom unites all Americans in a particular and unique way.

The final, culminating statement of the Constitution's Preamble set the goal for the new US government as that of securing "the blessings of Liberty to ourselves and our posterity." While condemning the US Constitution for failing to live up to this aim, the abolitionist William Lloyd Garrison began publishing *The Liberator* in 1831 to work for the achievement of freedom by other means. The Statue of Liberty is the recognized symbol of "the American Dream" to immigrants, signifying the freedom to succeed in accordance with work and ability. The white "Sons of Liberty" were succeeded by the Black "Freedom Riders" of the civil rights movement. The Freedom Train traveled throughout the United States in 1947 as an exhibition of documents and artifacts representing American history and identity. It was conceived as a way of celebrating and reinforcing the American attachment to freedom in the aftermath of the fight against Hitler's tyranny in Europe. In this time of legal segregation, viewing the train was an intentionally desegregated event—the train skipped the cities of Birmingham, Alabama, and Memphis, Tennessee, when local officials refused to allow white and Black Americans to view the train's collection at the same time. Homer Plessy's train allowed for racial division, but the Freedom Train would not.

The third American historical narrative, the narrative capable of breaking the impasse between the MR and US versions, is the narrative of Human Freedom (HF). The HF narrative can accommodate the honesty of the US narrative without falling prey to cynicism. It can also accommodate the inspirational dimension of the MR narrative without falling prey to triumphalism. It can be inclusive in a way that neither the US nor the MR versions can. In each of these ways, the HF narrative can also be a more accurate version of American history from the perspective of historical "fact." Apart from any particular narrative perspective one might adopt, the HF account is the one with the most clear and pervasive support in the historical record. Historical fact itself won't tell us which was more important, Abraham Lincoln or the Freedom Riders. MR thinks Lincoln from its narrative perspective, and US thinks Freedom Riders from its perspective. But HF reaches behind both Lincoln and the Freedom Riders to the concept of human freedom that played a central role for both.

The HF narrative of American history is not really a new idea, but it is one that has almost entirely disappeared from our national vision over the last half century or more. Its disappearance seems to have coincided roughly with the increasing political polarization and social fragmentation of the post–civil rights era. As competing groups have increasingly sought American historical narratives that are more narrowly tailored to their political objectives or identities, partial narratives like the MR and US ones have crowded out potential common ground narratives like HF. As a result of this—precisely because it is unsuitable as a weapon for internal conflicts—the HF narrative has not so much been rejected as forgotten.

The lens of human freedom makes sense of the American story. It allows for the simultaneous expression of unity and diversity characteristic of American identity—*e pluribus unum*—as no other concept or perspective does. The exercise of freedom, and the intense desire to recover it when it is lost, unites all human beings and distinguishes humans as a species from all other beings on earth.[17] The openness of American identity to anyone regardless of race, ethnicity, national origin, or religion is a function of this fact. If the American story is the story of human freedom, it is accessible to all human beings. At the same time that freedom accommodates diversity within this underlying unity, it also encourages the ongoing development of diversity. The exercise of freedom inevitably leads to a wide variety of different opinions, pursuits, life choices, and associations.

James Madison counted on this when he developed his plan for the "extended republic" in the most famous of the *Federalist Papers, Federalist* 10. "Liberty," according to Madison, is "essential to political life." The protection of this liberty by the government would ensure that a multiplicity of "factions" would develop throughout the United States. The greater the number of these factions, the less likely it would be that any of them would become a national majority and tyrannize over the others. The exercise of human freedom would naturally lead to a diversity of opinions and interests, and this diversity would itself assist in protecting freedom for all.

It is sometimes said that as Americans we can find unity in our diversity. On its face, this is pure nonsense. Unity and diversity are direct definitional opposites. We might as well try finding harmony in dissonance or love in hatred. What is really meant by this—or what should be meant if it is to make sense—is that we Americans can find unity in our commitment to human freedom, which is both compatible with and productive of diversity in other areas. Diversity is valuable and beautiful as the varied representation of humanity, and as the natural outgrowth of the freedom that makes humans so interesting and important. There is nothing inherently good or bad about difference itself. Difference is a brute fact. Diversity within humanity, on the other hand, is a shining symbol of the freedom that makes individuals unique while uniting us all.

The unity that Americans can find in freedom is on particular display in the case of white and Black Americans. The struggle by African Americans for the exercise of freedom throughout American history resonates directly with the motivation of the first white European settlers in North America, and with their subsequent experience up to and including the War for Independence from Great Britain. The early European settlers went to incredible lengths to obtain freedom from the oppressive religious, political, and economic structures of Europe. The voyage across the Atlantic Ocean was long and dangerous. What lay on the other end of the journey was largely unknown. Once arrived, survival was often precarious and dependent on the constant, laborious exercise of freedom both personal and political. The force of the desire for freedom that drove the early European colonists out of Europe and into North America was one of the most powerful examples of human exertion in history.

This force continued to motivate subsequent generations of European North Americans, who carried the momentum of westward migration from the ocean across the land. "Manifest Destiny" was continuous with European North American settlement; the same desire for freedom that animated settlement on the east coast also drove later immigrants and future generations across the continent. To say that a human desire for freedom drove early settlement and westward expansion is not by any means to deny the often morally reprehensible outgrowths of these movements. The desire to dominate and subjugate is a common pathology of the unregulated desire for freedom. When the drive to be free becomes unmoored from the moral respect due to the freedom of others, freedom for oneself quickly transforms into tyranny over others. This is what happened in the case of European-American tyranny over Native American people as well as enslaved African Americans. An extreme desire for freedom was transmogrified into an appetite for domination.

The trajectory of the white European North American freedom struggle reached its apex in the Revolutionary War. By 1787, the historian David Ramsay could already complain in his *History of the American Revolution* that American culture had deteriorated significantly, perhaps irrevocably.[18] Early Americans had begun the inexorable process of becoming their erstwhile enemies. When the struggle for freedom effectively ended, the more difficult work of maintaining freedom began. Frequent renewal efforts would be needed to restore the appreciation for human freedom that drains from established societies like sand through a sieve.

This is precisely what the African American struggle for freedom has provided for all Americans from that time to our own. Black Americans have always fought, as Nikole Hannah-Jones has said, to make American ideals of freedom true. We interpret this statement to mean that since 1776 (or even earlier), Black Americans have picked up the standard of the very same idea of human freedom that inspired the early white European Americans to declare independence from Great Britain. For these white Americans, the ideal of human freedom had already begun to be tainted by the increasing institutionalization of slavery throughout the colonies and in the early United States. The pure ideal of freedom had been thoroughly mixed with the poison of domination.

The cause of securing freedom for enslaved African Americans has carried the torch of the true American story ever since. The apex of the white European American struggle for freedom marked the launching point of the African American struggle for freedom. The work of refining American freedom and restoring it to its rightful place at the center of American life has been the joint work of white and Black Americans from that time to ours. The cause of racial justice is the cause of American freedom continued and purified.

Numerous other racial, ethnic, and immigrant groups have made vital contributions to the American story of human freedom. This story can't be told only in Black and white.[19] But if the HF narrative of American history is true, its central drama lies in the conjoined historical arcs of the European American and African American freedom struggles.

MR, US, HF

Everybody likes freedom—especially we Americans who profess to live in "the land of the free." But as a central ideal in the American conversation, freedom has fallen off the radar screen in recent decades.[20] This demotion has played an important role in our collective alienation from our national history, and in the disintegration of our national unity of purpose. The freedom vs. slavery dichotomy had driven the most consequential events in American history. Without human freedom as our national star and compass, we have gone adrift.

The US version of American history prioritizes at least a handful of concepts or ideals above freedom. Equality, justice, multiculturalism, and other concepts all outrank freedom on the US account. This is partly a consequence of the centrality of freedom to traditionally mainstream American historical texts. It is also a consequence of the poisoning effect of enslavement on early white European American embraces of freedom. Freedom can seem like one of the "master's tools" that the US account often deems unsuitable for dismantling the "master's house." Freedom has been a central component of versions of American history that have already been told. It has coexisted with tyranny and oppression of Native American and African American people. Because of this, proponents of the US narrative have not prioritized freedom as a leading concept.

The MR narrative of American history initially seems to have a more prominent place for freedom. "Freedom isn't free" is a slogan frequently touted by its proponents in support of the US military. But the MR narrative doesn't have much use for freedom as an ideal either. This narrative foregrounds individuals, great events, and concrete symbols over abstract ideals. The guiding motivations of individuals like Thomas Jefferson, James Madison, Alexander Hamilton, or George Washington have been eclipsed by their shining achievements. We have the Declaration of Independence, the Constitution, the Flag, the National Anthem, the Emancipation Proclamation, and other notable monuments to American achievement and progress.[21] The freedom struggles of early European Americans have been all but lost to the American public consciousness, and the freedom struggles of African Americans were completed with the 13th Amendment, or at least the civil rights movement. Freedom is more "mission accomplished" than a living struggle, according to the MR narrative.

To say that freedom hasn't been a primary component of either the MR or US versions of American history is not to say that it has been completely abandoned. Freedom still resonates in various ways with both. But allowing human freedom to shape our telling of the American Story as a whole provides a more honest, inspiring, and inclusive American historical narrative than either the MR or US versions can.

The American story as the story of human freedom is more honest than the alternatives because it encourages both (1) a direct reckoning with the history of enslavement as the antithesis of freedom, and (2) an accurate evaluation of the motivating ideals of the most consequential events in American history, from settlement to the present. Foregrounding freedom reveals the sheer extent and depth of the evil of slavery. It exposes the "necessary evil" argument of the American Founders—the argument favored by the MR narrative—as false on its face. The antithesis of the American story cannot be necessary to it.

At the same time, the HF narrative is honest in its assessment of the importance of American achievements throughout our history. The American story has often been a force for progress, both within the United States and around the world. From the Revolutionary War to the Civil War, World War II, and the Cold War, the United States has often (though of course not always) framed its involvement in conflicts as struggles for human freedom. And these struggles have, in fact, coincided with significant advances for human freedom both within the United States and throughout the world over the past 250 years. Contrary to the MR narrative, the great individuals and national symbols involved in these struggles have been freedom's mere vessels. Without the cause of human freedom, their historical importance vanishes.

The HF version of the American story is more inspiring than the alternatives because it includes both a moral baseline and a lofty aim. Related concepts of equality or justice express baseline moral demands—fixed standards that are either achieved or not. Equality and justice may be approached more or less closely, but at the end of the day they are either present or absent. Freedom is different. Freedom includes a moral baseline defined by the absence of slavery: freedom from slavery or coercion by another. But freedom also admits of degrees defined by its objects or goals: freedom to express and fulfill one's humanity. This two-sided nature of freedom—freedom from and freedom to—makes freedom a more dynamic, uplifting, and inspiring concept than these others.

The American story as the story of human freedom is also more inclusive than either the MR or US versions. The MR version tends to exclude, neglect, or demote those who have been historically excluded, neglected, or demoted from full participation in American political life. It mirrors the concrete power relations of American social and political history. The US version tends to do the opposite. It uplifts and emphasizes those whom the MR version excludes or neglects. The HF version avoids both forms of partiality, equally including and emphasizing both those historically included and those historically excluded. The theme of HF equally embraces both those who enjoy it and those who are struggling to achieve it. It can be a pat on the back, a fire in the belly, or a kick in the pants. In this way HF includes both those upheld by the MR version of American history and those upheld by the US version. It includes both freedom achieved and freedom denied.

DU BOIS, DOUBLE CONSCIOUSNESS, AND BLACK MUSIC

This dynamic of freedom is nowhere expressed more profoundly and beautifully than in the philosophy and art of the African diaspora. Perhaps one of the most wonderful utterances on the notion of freedom appears in *The World and Africa* by William Edward Burghardt Du Bois:

I dream of a world of infinite and invaluable variety; In a realm of "true freedom" in thought and dream, fantasy and imagination; in gift, aptitude, and genius—all possible manner of difference, topped

with freedom of soul to do and be, and freedom of thought to give
to a world and build into it, all wealth of inborn individuality. Each
effort to stop this freedom of being is a blow at democracy. . . . There
can be no perfect democracy curtailed by color, race, or poverty.[22]

Du Bois's vision of a free world has not yet been realized. Despite all the
work done by Du Bois and many Black activists and allies around the
world throughout the twentieth and into the twenty-first centuries, the
effects of global racism are still only too real. Consider the rise of the far
right across Europe, the baffling Brexit situation in England, the treatment of sub-Saharan African immigrants in the Middle East and Asia,
and of course, the underlying messages of hate and white supremacy in
more recent American political campaigns and policies.[23] These effects
are also clearly visible on the continent of Africa where men and women
are bleaching their skin in higher numbers than ever. This is a sad irony,
and stark evidence of an enduring racist view of dark skin. This trend is
also reflective of self-hatred, a psychological impact of colonialism and
imperialism.

The intellectual thought of W. E. B. Du Bois and the artistic reflections
and responses of Black musicians from opera singer Camilla Williams to
jazz drummer Max Roach shed much-needed light on the relationship of
global racism to the American story. In their own ways and through their
own media, these activists attempted to sound the alarm and illuminate
the shadows that obscure the reality of racism across the globe. Focusing
only on the United States without understanding the global history and
reach of white supremacy is like looking only at the trees and ignoring the
forest. Black American intellectuals and musicians of the twentieth century such as Du Bois, Williams, and Roach help to illuminate this forest of
global racism. They show that Race and the American Story is best understood by examining race and the global story.

Black folks have struggled for centuries against white supremacy in
Africa and across the diaspora, including the United States. This common
struggle has, however, encountered obstacles to its success in the division
between certain parts of the diaspora. Saying that there is a rift between

Africans and African Americans is not saying anything new. This rift has been driven by decades of misinformation and miseducation, resulting in misunderstanding and mistrust. In 2019, for instance, there were a number of instances that excavated that chasm—the news that Harriet Tubman would be played by a Nigerian-British woman had Black Twitter in a tizzy about the so-called Nigerian take-over, because weren't all the major actors in *Get-Out* and *Selma* also Nigerians?

This rift is exacerbated by the American descendants of slavery (ADOS) rhetoric about who should receive reparations. Their apparent leaning toward what some may interpret as xenophobic anti-immigration policies is deeply divisive and worrying. In principle, ADOS has excellent goals that are unquestionable; reparations, if ever attained, must go only to American descendants of slavery. It is the effect of this rhetorical advocacy on their tenuous relationship with other Black folks in the United States that is worrying. One of the better responses to ADOS was offered by socially conscious African American rapper Talib Kweli in an eloquent essay on *Medium*. He concludes, "ADOS is a danger to actual Black activists who have been active in the fight for reparations."[24]

As early as 1946, W. E. B. Du Bois anticipated this condition of the Black world in an essay titled "American Negroes and Africa," where he pointed to the fact that "one of the curious results of current fear and hysteria is the breaking of ties between Africa and American Negroes."[25] He was describing the difficulties he and other Pan-Africanists had encountered as they were trying to arrange a fifth meeting of the Pan-African congress. He lamented that "this current story gets small space in Afro-American press."[26] The field of Africana Studies stands at a precarious point where it must consider new ways to bridge the gap.

Du Bois had an expansive view of the Black world that allows us to stretch the corners of the "vast veil" that he so eloquently described in *The Souls of Black Folk*, as shutting us out of "the other world." When Du Bois visited the poverty-stricken Black community in rural Tennessee, he described "the veil that hung between us and Opportunity." This is relevant for both Africans and African Americans as we contend with the effects of postcolonial imperialism on the motherland and of the legacies of slavery in the United States. In Africa this takes the form of World Bank and International Monetary Fund austerity measures, widespread corruption, misappropriated and ill-fitting models of Western political, economic, and religious institutions, and the psychological effects of years of Western cultural hegemony. In the United States this manifests in racial disparities in education, healthcare, housing, incarceration rates, and the enduring pervasive psychological state of generational racism that manifests every day in landmark, newsworthy events and in casual everyday life.

These oppressive forces of white supremacy erode the wholeness that could be Black life in the Motherland and in the United States, in both gradual shifts and in avalanches. Throughout his career, Du Bois gave great attention to Africa, which was evident in his publications, from his 1915 book *The Negro*, to his 1946 book *The World and Africa*, and beyond. In the latter, Du Bois expands the corners of the veil created by white supremacy in Africa. He berates "the doctrine of the Superior Race: the theory that a minority of the people of Europe are by birth and natural gift the rulers of mankind; rulers of their own suppressed labor classes and, without doubt, heaven-sent rulers of yellow, brown, and Black people."[27] He goes on to explain that "The word 'Negro' was used for the first time in the world's history to tie color to race and Blackness to slavery and degradation. The white race was pictured as 'pure' and superior; the Black race as dirty, stupid, and inevitably inferior. . . . Everything great, fine, and really successful in human culture was white."[28]

Du Bois's Pan-African vision began, however, as a particularly American concept. In his most famous book, *The Souls of Black Folk*, he declares that "the problem of the twentieth century is the problem of the color line." The "color line" contributes to the definition of what Du Bois calls the "double consciousness" of African Americans. Du Bois's theory of double-consciousness is pivotal to understanding the psychological realities of the African American experience. DuBois argued that the Negro was best understood as an individual with two streams of influence—the African and the American. In *The Souls of Black Folk* (1903) he states, "One ever feels his twoness—an American, a Negro; two souls, two thoughts, two unreconciled strivings; two warring ideals in one dark body, whose dogged strength alone keeps it from being torn asunder."[29]

This "twoness" is exhibited in a particularly clear way in the position of Black classical music composers and artists. DuBois's theory addresses the unique position of the Black performer in classical music and explains the tendency for them to retain their vernacular expressions while choosing to expand their musical repertoire with classical music training. As many scholars have recognized, this merging of African American and European influences distinguished the vitality of the classical music created and performed by African Americans.[30]

An excellent and early example of this is found in the work of Samuel Coleridge-Taylor. British-born Coleridge-Taylor (b. 1875) was one of the first Black composers to gain wide acclaim for his works, notably *Hiawatha's Wedding Feast* (1898). He incorporated elements from Negro folk musical tradition in his original compositions and created new arrangements as illustrated in *African Suite* (1898), *Twenty-Four Negro Melodies* (1905), and his *Concerto in G Major* (1911).[31]

Other Black composers merged their two streams of influence in their compositions. For instance, William Grant Still (b. 1895), known as the "Dean of Afro-American Composers," is noted as the first Black composer to have symphonic work performed by a major American symphony. His *Afro-American Symphony*, described as reflecting two lineages—African American and European—was performed in Philadelphia in 1931.[32] In this work and other works, he used Negro folk music—specifically spirituals and blues. Similar to many Black musicians of his era, Still became acquainted with Black vernacular expressions as a child, recalling: "My maternal grandmother lived with us in Little Rock until her death and I remember her singing about the house all the time, singing spirituals and hymns"[33] He was successful not only as an African American composer but also as an American composer and he was the first African American to conduct a major symphony orchestra.

William Grant Still's contributions represent a significant shift in America's reception of the Black composer. Still drew from these vernac-ular resources to write a body of Black nationalistic music over a period of fifteen years including *La Guiblesse* (1926) and *Africa* (1930) (Gillum 1943: 179–180; Southern 1997: 432). Still's far-reaching appeal was evident in a critic's review in the *San Diego Union* of August 1938:

> That concert was more than music. It sliced a memorable cross-section through the big, complicated, only half appreciated setup which we casually define as American. The evening's podium responsibilities were shared by the German-born Julius Leib and the Negro composer-conductor, William Grant Still. . . . None of us knows whether the music of William Grant Still is going to last ten years, or fifty, or five hundred . . . [but] let us step forward and state that—here and now, in the year of 1938—"Kaintuck" is a work of haunting loveliness and "Lenox Avenue" is spine-tingling stuff. These rhythms are the rhythms of our time, and these astringent harmonies are a musical speech to which we respond.[34]

Other African American composers who displayed the double consciousness of their identities in their works include Harry T. Burleigh (b. 1866), R. Nathaniel Dett (b. 1882), Florence Price (b. 1888), John W. Work (b. 1901), Hall Smith (b. 1925), Julia Perry (b. 1927), Noel Da-Costa (b. 1930), Coleridge-Taylor Perkinson (b.1932), and Olly Wilson (b. 1937). Olly Wilson describes the musical tradition as being "characterized by a greater interaction and interpenetration of African and Euro-American elements"[35] Wilson played for the church Sunday school for years, and this impacted his work, which was also influenced by Stravinsky and Schoenberg.[36] African American composers continued to use folk music to varying degrees depending on the individual composer. The works of African American composers assumed a stature and influence that was comparable to the works of any other renowned composer in the field. Hall Smith is quoted in Raoul Abdul's *Blacks in Classical Music* (1977) as saying: "Place our works on programs with Beethoven, Mozart, Schoenberg, Copland, and the current avant-gardists. We don't even have to be called 'Black.' When we stand for our bows, that fact will become clear when it should: after the work has made its own impact."

Using Du Bois's theory of double-consciousness as a framework for interpreting the creative activities of African American composers as well as singers and instrumentalists associated with European concert forms allows for a more nuanced critique of the contributions to this tradition. Du Bois seems to imply that African Americans could have one foot in Black culture and the other in mainstream American culture. Arnold Rampersad suggests that part of Du Bois's concept was drawn from the field of psychology and the problem of the split personality.[37] I would instead amend the concept slightly and advocate that these artists stand with both feet on one ground, embracing the dual nature of their African heritage and American nationality.

This stance was not always balanced for African American artists. Black poet and writer Amiri Baraka eloquently explained in his autobiography his attraction to one part of his identity: "[I] was stretched between two lives and perceptions (I've told you it was four—Black, Brown, Yellow, White—but actually its two on the realest side, the two extremes), the Black and the White, . . . Black people surrounded me. And that was the element I felt easiest in."[38]

Baraka obviously felt more drawn to the African heritage portion of his identity. Conversely, Paul Lawrence Dunbar emphasized the American heritage element when he wrote, "For 250 years, the environment of the Negro has been American, in every respect the same as that of all other Americans."[39] African American performers of art music stand in the same world as Baraka and Dunbar. These performers used, to the best of their ability, the creative, musical, and intellectual material available to them as both American and African American.

Therefore, to relegate African Americans to a designated "Black" box of expressive culture is to deny them the vast scope of the dual nature of their identity—African heritage and American nationality. Although of African heritage, they are also Americans who have at their disposal all the cultural expressions created and expressed in America. For decades, Black scholars and intellectuals have debated extensively about the specific cultural pool (African or mainstream American) that should serve as creative inspiration for African American musicians, writers, and performers.

In the early twentieth century, Booker T. Washington and W. E. B. Du Bois grappled with the functional definition of the scholastic and economic interests of the African American community. Booker T. Washington insisted that the education the Negro needed should be devoted more to vocational training than to the arts or humanities that W. E. B. Du Bois emphasized. Washington suggested that the generation of Black youth seeking education in the early part of the century should not venture toward the arts, for what was needed in the Black community was "a firm [economic] foundation"[40] (1974:373). Washington questioned the need for any education that was not immediately convertible to Black economic empowerment. As early as in an 1896 article, Washington explained that "someone may be tempted to ask, Has not the negro boy or girl as good a right to study French grammar and instrumental music as the white youth? Yes, but in the present condition of the negro race in this country there is need of something more."[41]

Du Bois, on the other hand, encouraged those Blacks who were capable to reach "higher" for culture, arts and humanities. He envisioned that a new Black vanguard, "emancipated by training and culture"[42], armed and accomplished in the white man's knowledge, would form the bedrock of future Black leadership. This group would lead the masses to a better life and means of existence.[43] Du Bois's journal, *Crisis*, became an avenue for the promotion of literature, arts, theater, and other artistic expressions that were, he urged, important for the Black vanguard to grasp. This select group widely known as the "talented 10th" or "the upper-tens" evolved into a group that was distinct from the masses of African Americans.

Professionally, Black performers who thrived in classical music could fit into this group of "upper tens" because their choices of artistic expression, the European musical material and style, were clear examples of what Du Bois, Locke, and other "renaissance men and women" advocated. The cultural revolution of the Harlem Renaissance encouraged Black artists to "cross the essentialist color line"[44] According to Samuel A. Floyd, "the primary motive of the movement was political: if African Americans could demonstrate substantial abilities in arts and letters, then social, political, and economic freedoms would surely follow."[45] Indeed, Black performers were now encouraged to step out of what was considered the musical and artistic boundaries of "Black culture" and venture into areas that were, for the most part, exclusive to white people. Du Bois and others insisted that this "New Negro" was to be "elevated" in his way of life and his art.

The effects of this movement were far reaching across the country and across the artistic forms of literature, visual art, theater and music. Art music became an important musical expression for the "New Negro" and suited the new elitist and intellectual ideologies that the movement espoused. Also, the Harlem Renaissance showed the rest of the world that this "New Negro" could celebrate the wealth of his Black heritage as well as give outstanding performances on the concert stage in the same way that a handful of African American composers had displayed their talents at the turn of the century.

The Black concert performers who carried the Harlem Renaissance torch and responded to Alain Locke's insistence that "a great folk music demands a great classical music" (1936) crossed racial barriers to participate in classical music. They have sometimes been overlooked and omitted from Black music historiographies[46] because they are perhaps perceived to have exited the "Black" musical tradition. However, during this period of the1920s and beyond, these Black concert performers answered the call of Black activism in their own way. The concert singers included more Negro folk songs in their repertoires, and the composers incorporated Negro folk themes in their compositions.[47] Like other concert artists, Camilla Williams—who was the subject of my dissertation—consistently included spirituals in her concert programs. This ability to combine and juxtapose western European and African American musical traditions showed the white audiences and critics that Black artists were not restricted to the usual "Black musical forms," but could draw on them to enhance and flavor their own classical music compositions and performances. The realization of this feat revealed that Black classical artists could indeed occupy a deserving place among Black artists regardless of the musical tradition they had opted to embrace. Indeed, Spencer sees the achievements of individuals like William Grant Still, Dorothy Maynor, and R. Nathaniel Dett as being central to the philosophy of the Harlem Renaissance.

Black performers of classical music embraced what Alain Locke referred to as "a separate strand of music" (1936), the American component of their heritage, which was distinct from the tradition associated with the "core Black culture." Samuel Floyd describes this "core culture" as that portion of the Black population ... whose primary cultural values and interests lie *within* that community."[48] The Black classical artists began their careers in the earlier part of the twentieth century (some even before) when the arguments between Washington and Du Bois were perhaps most compelling. Washington would probably have queried the use these artists would be to their fledgling Black communities. Washington would have argued that these artists could not, from the concert stage, positively impact the balance sheets and the economic fortunes of their families. Indeed, Washington pondered in his 1896 article, the financial implications of these Black artists' escapades on their families' resources. He suggested that precious dollars were being diverted from what were considered to be important vocational pursuits and allocated to piano, voice, and other lessons as well as for instrument rentals. Indeed, Camilla Williams tells of the financial burden that this path cost her and her family. For a girl from a working-class family, voice lessons were expensive. She had to rely on generous benefactors to carry her talent along to a point where it could take off into a successful career. Williams and other artists in this unfamiliar field persisted somehow and excelled in the type of music that Du Bois and other exponents of the Harlem Renaissance artistic movement advocated.

Interestingly, the careers of many of these Black artists who created and performed art music thrived in Harlem, New York. Harlem was a hub of activity for the writers and the artists of this intellectual and artistic group. One of the literary voices of this "New Negro" movement, Arna Bontemps, fondly describes New York as a place "devoid of racial convulsions. New York became a locus for what I would regard as a more exciting and perhaps more telling assault on oppression than the dreary blood-in-the-streets strategy of preceding years."[49] Although Camilla Williams grew up in the South, her career took off after she moved to the East Coast, first to Philadelphia, and then to New York.

The classical artists' "assault" on the race problem involved strategies with which these artists would prove to the world the high caliber of their craftsmanship and their devotion to artistic excellence. The education that this select group of African Americans attained often placed them in that cohort we now consider the "Black elite" or "Black bourgeoisie." According to Gatewood Brown, "the genteel performance" exhibited by these Black elite artists distinguished them from the masses of uneducated lower-class Blacks.[50] While skin shade/color and money were further qualifications to be a Black elite, education was certainly the main criterion. Historian Leslie H. Fishel Jr. reflects that "the Black elite were assimilationists believing that as whites recognized their high cultural standards and gentility, the barriers to interracial activities for the Black aristocracy would diminish."[51] One may argue that the associations that Camilla Williams made with the Black elite in Philadelphia contributed to her entry into the world of opera. Her crossover to the western European musical world was mediated by the Black elite with whom she interacted.

Some commentators on this Black elite/bourgeoisie issue adopted more vehement tones in their criticism. Sociologist E. Franklin Frazier thoroughly described and analyzed the Black bourgeoisie in his book of the same title. While he recognized the important position this small powerful group had as a part of the larger Black community, in the final analysis, he ridiculed their image and legacy: "The Black bourgeoisie suffers from 'nothingness' because when negroes attain middle-class status, their lives generally lose both content and significance."[52]

Many Black intellectuals of the Harlem Renaissance and beyond would disagree with Frazier's position. Alain Locke, W. E. B. Du Bois and others expected the elite Black artists to transform Black artistic expression into "higher" forms.[53] For instance, the Negro spirituals were to be arranged in a manner consistent with European musical standards. The leaders of the talented tenth argued that this would elevate the spiritual to a level compatible with existing Western concert music. While such Harlem Renaissance artists as Langston Hughes and Zora Neale Hurston insisted that the Black forms were just as good if they were left in their original vernacular forms,[54] the "elevation" school of thought certainly convinced many to reach for what was considered a higher level of life and expression. Consequently Black composers of art and classical music in the twentieth century—from William Grant Still to Regina Harris Baiocchi—adapted to the European classical musical style and format, while singers and instrumentalists spent many years and abundant financial resources perfecting their voices and instruments to be acceptable to European standards.

The "elevation" school of thought and its "talented tenth" concept seems to have had influence with Camilla Williams. For instance, she disliked the portrayal of Blacks in the folk opera *Porgy and Bess* because they were portrayed in what she thought to be a "low-down manner." Blacks, she said, had risen above the image of a bunch of street Negroes shooting crap and living "like that." In the same manner, Ms. Williams preferred straightened hair to ethnic braids and hairstyles. Although her passion for classical and art music is without doubt, Williams was never drawn to the other popular musical genres that were created by African Americans, such as funk, soul, and rhythm and blues.

It would be reasonable to speculate that these examples indicate Ms. Williams's eligibility for classification as belonging to the "upper tens" group described by DuBois and Willard Gatewood. Another compelling fact to consider is that many Black women who gained success on the concert stage or in opera married European or white American men. One might postulate that these women were attempting to embrace the overwhelmingly white worldview, thereby elevating or partially extricating themselves from the Black culture in which they had been nurtured.

What can be deduced from this situation? Where do these artists belong in American culture? Although artists like Camilla Williams clearly drew inspiration from contemporary American national culture, there were also many ways in which Ms. Williams also revealed her stable grounding in Black culture—whether it was her love for a special dish she calls "nigger soup" or her passion for the advancement of younger Black people irrespective of their chosen career.

Whether one argues that the artists who emerged were members of the Black middle class, the Black elite, the Negro genius (as Benjamin

Brawley calls them), or part of the Black bourgeoisie, the double consciousness that constituted the essence of their cultural expressions and the professions they chose cannot be overemphasized. At least as much as any Black artist who ventured into the Black musical genres like blues and jazz, these classical music performers exemplified the coming together of the two streams of consciousness that run through the souls of African Americans.

MAX ROACH AND GLOBAL RACISM

Although the work of jazz drummer Max Roach might be traced to the intellectual foundations of W. E. B. Du Bois, their proximity might be traced to the late 1950s, when Max Roach and vocalist Abbey Lincoln became involved in the American Society of African Culture (AMSAC). According to Ian Rocksborough-Smith, AMSAC was "formed as a think tank of mainly university-educated, liberal, and moderately left-leaning African American intellectuals based in Washington, DC."[55] It was to be "a space, however ideologically circumscribed, through which transatlantic discussion about colonialism could continue." Rocksborough Smith explains that "Du Bois' academic accomplishments and ideas were widely recognized, if contentiously debated, in the circle of academics who headed AMSAC. Such contentions highlighted the divided terrain of Cold War racial politics in the Black community."[56] This is the keenly interrogative atmosphere within which Max Roach and Abbey Lincoln created some of their most political work.

Indeed, throughout the 1950s, African Americans contended with hundreds of atrocities, among them the killing of Emmett Till in 1955 and the Alabama church bombing in 1958. In 1959, Max Roach and lyricist Oscar Brown Jr. began to work on a collaborative project to respond to their own historical moment. They were also inspired to prepare for the celebration of the centennial of the Emancipation Proclamation which would take place in 1963. But in 1960, Roach decided to release the project as a musical and artistic response to the ugliness of segregation and racism. *We*

Insist: Max Roach's Freedom Now Suite was released by Candid Records in 1960.[57] Other collaborators on the album include percussionist Babatunde Olatunji, saxophonists Coleman Hawkins and Walter Benton, trumpeter Booker Little, trombonist Julian Priester, and most importantly, Roach's then girlfriend, vocalist Abbey Lincoln. According to jazz scholar Ingrid Monson, this album "is perhaps the best-known jazz work with explicitly political content."[58]

Before and since then, Black artists around the world have used their platforms to create music that fights back against white supremacist systems of power and pathological narratives of oppression. However, I want to posit that the *We Insist* album is a unique and critical album because it reflects two important aspects of Black life: liberation and love. These two subjects are at the heart of every movement that Black people have embarked on, and yet they are not often paired in one text, certainly not when that text emerges from a complicated genre like jazz. But *We Insist* offers a nuanced understanding of these two subjects.

In terms of Black *liberation*, artists often zoom in on one part of the Black world, one region, or one subgroup of Black people at one time: Curtis Mayfield focused on the United States of the 1970s, Fela Anikulapo Kuti on postindependent Nigeria, Hugh Masekela on South Africa, Kendrick Lamar and Janelle Monet on twenty-first-century youth in urban United States. Max Roach's *We Insist* album does all of this by covering time and space. It stretches back to slavery and reaches out from the United States back to Africa and looms over the entire continent.

In 1958, before composing *We Insist*, Max Roach and bass player Oscar Pettiford joined saxophonist Sonny Rollins on his nineteen-minute-long *Freedom Suite*. The composition is stark, with only sax, bass and drums. If the music did not convey his intent, Rollins explains the inspiration in his liner notes: "America is deeply rooted in Negro culture: its colloquialisms; its humor; its music. How ironic that the Negro, who more than any other people can claim America's culture as his own, is being persecuted and repressed; that the Negro, who has exemplified the humanities in his very existence, is being rewarded with inhumanity."

Uncomfortable with this statement, the white owner of Riverside Records, Orrin Keepnews, renamed the piece ("Shadow Waltz") and wrote a different explanation for the liner notes: "This suite, then is 'about' Sonny Rollins: more precisely, it is about freedom as Sonny is equipped to perceive it. . . . In one sense, then, the reference is to the musical freedom of this unusual combination of composition and improvisation; in another it is to physical and moral freedom, to the presence and absence of it in Sonny's own life and in the way of life of other Americans to whom he feels a relationship." This is a very ambiguous and equivocal explanation that lays no responsibility on the oppressors but instead turns the spotlight back on the oppressed, as if what Rollins is dealing with here is all in his head.

There is no such ambiguity in *We Insist!* In 1958, the same year as Rollins's album, perhaps musing on what he learned in that collaboration, Max Roach was featured on the cover of *DownBeat* magazine. In the interview, he said, "I hope to write some things that mean something, some larger works than those I've done." Even though the *We Insist* album was released in 1960, it conceptually frames time—almost four centuries—and space beginning with slavery in 1619 and ending in Johannesburg, South Africa, in the 1990s. With five tracks, Roach adopts a Pan-African vision of the Black world reminiscent of Du Bois. Track 1, "Driva Man," has a work song vibe and is set during slavery; Track 2, "Freedom Day," is about the confusion of Juneteenth; Track 4, "All Africa," strides across the Atlantic to celebrate independence and sovereignty as Abbey and Nigerian drummer Babatunde Olatunji chant the names of thirty-six African tribes; and track 5, "Tears for Johannesburg," reminds us of the harsh injustices of apartheid. The pivotal moment of the album is the third track, the bridge between the past and the future, the Americas and the Motherland. It allows us to focus on the intersectional journeys of Black women and presents us with the complexities of romantic Black love, the tensions that exist between Black men and women, and the distinct burdens they carry in a society that encouraged and urged fractures in the relationship since slavery.

The track is called "Triptych: Prayer, Protest, Peace," and is the most poignant and striking piece on the album. If the four other tracks tell the story of the history of Black experiences, this third track tells the story of the internal psyche and trauma that these peoples have endured. In his book *In the Break*, Fred Moten describes this break, this important juncture on this album,: "Lincoln hums and then screams over Roach's increasingly and insistently intense percussion, moving inexorably in a trajectory and towards a location that is remote from—if not in excess of or inaccessible to—words."[59]

In 1957, three years before the *We Insist* album, Abbey Lincoln released the album *That's Him*. On it was the song "Strong Man," which Oscar Brown Jr. wrote to capture her love of Roach. Ingrid Monson explains that "Brown met Abbey Lincoln when she was performing at the Black Orchid in Chicago in 1957. At her request he wrote the song 'Strong Man' for her then boyfriend Max Roach." "Strong Man" is a tender song about this wonderful Black man she is deeply in love with: "what a hardworking hero is he/with dark and shining arms, crisp curly hair/lips warm and full." This was a rare picture of Black love. Roach and Lincoln would later get married in 1962. Since Oscar Brown wrote this specifically for Lincoln about Max, we might understand the extent to which she threw herself into the *We Insist* project three years later. Most critics agree that Abbey Lincoln brought an urgency to the album, particularly in the *Triptych* track, that set it apart from the rest of the jazz albums of that time, making it very different even from Sonny Rollins's *Freedom Suite*.

In "Triptych," Abbey Lincoln vocalizes the deep painful experience of being a Black woman. The song is divided into three parts: Prayer, Protest, Peace. When I listen to this, I am transported to the belly of the slave ship, the earnest reach for a spiritual power that will lead us out, the deep moans and screams of anger and distress, and the yearning for peace. But I understand this personally too because I am moved to Prayer, Protest and Peace every time I or my children, or my husband encounter racism or sexism, the results of slavery, colonialism, imperialism.

Fred Moten likens the sound of Lincoln in "Protest" to the beating of Frederick Douglass's Aunt Hester. Of "Protest," Moten says, "The revolution embedded in such duration is, for a moment, a run of questions: What is the edge of this event? What am I, the object? What is the music? What is manhood? What is the feminine? What is the beautiful? What will Blackness be?"[60] All this is conveyed in the "Protest" section of Triptych. Aida Mbowa explains that "Abbey Lincoln screams. A scream can be a literal testimony of a body in physical pain. In Black history to scream is to defy silencing, and the attempt to erase the very human and necessary noise in response to physical injury—to whips, to smacks, to the breaking of the body."[61] Mbowa insists that these screams are an embodiment of the pain from slavery onwards. It is language without words. What, she asks, are the "political repercussions of an inability to express pain?" How often do we go through our days silently, unable to utter the frustration, exhaustion, pain and shock when those waves hit us?

Max Roach's foray into Africa on the last two tracks qualifies this album further as an Africana studies text because it connects the story in the Americas to the story of Africa. It reminds us that oppression and power of white supremacy has manifested in different parts of the Black world. "All Africa" captures the story of independence and sovereignty across the continent of Africa. After the continent was divided up by Europe at the Berlin Conference of 1884, the different regions spent decades working to reclaim their independence. Some of these movements yielded bloody wars and others were won by diplomacy. From the 1950s to the 1990s, African countries triumphed, throwing off the shackles of colonialism but embroiled in the continual struggle to decipher their own identities after the such long encounters with the oppressor and their European trappings such as language and educational systems. For "All Africa," Nigerian drummer Babatunde Olatunji accompanies Abbey Lincoln on polyrhythmic conga drums and as she calls out thirty-six ethnic groups, he responds with Yoruba proverbs and other ethnic exclamations. It is significant that Lincoln starts with "Bantu," which is a language subgroup in sub-Saharan Africa spoken by over 85 million people, originating on the Cameroon/Nigeria border.

We know that the last bastions of colonial European dominance in Africa were in Zimbabwe and South Africa. The last track on the album, "Tears for Johannesburg," deals with the horrors of apartheid, which was in full force even as civil rights and Black power leaders were insisting of the dismantling of Jim Crow laws in the United States. As Abbey begins with cries and wordless calls for justice, freedom, and as Olatunji and Roach join her, we are reminded of the harsh history of apartheid.

In his autobiography, *The Beat of My Drum*, Babatunde Olatunji reflects on the relevance of this album, and his participation in it. Calling it an "anti-segregationist album," Olatunji explains that because of the album, "Max did not get that much support from club owners in those days. He was someone who went about his work and stuck to what he believed in." Indeed, Ingrid Monson asserts that a close look at this album reveals "the interplay between the social, the political and the musical [which] reminds us that jazz tradition has always been in dialogue with the social and cultural movements going on around it, and has often been at its most inspired when engaged in social commentary." Monson's view reminds us of Du Bois's thoughts on the importance of music for Black folks. He concludes his chapter on the sorrow Songs with this: "Through all the sorrow songs, there breathes a hope—a faith in the ultimate justice of things. The minor cadences of despair change often to triumph and calm confidence."[62] There is perhaps no better example of this than Max Roach's *Freedom Now Suite*.

CONCLUSION

When we were recently invited by a book club of about fifty elderly mostly white citizens in Missouri to lead a version of Race and the American Story, we wondered how the curriculum would translate to a different audience made of a generation that had lived through the civil rights movement. We pared down the readings for an eight-week study and allowed the small groups to read and discuss on their own. Adam and Stephanie joined the group at three points during the course—at the beginning, middle, and end. We introduced the course and laid out the rationale for the readings, then we returned to the full group at the end to pull together the strings of discussion. But it was our visit at the midpoint in the course that was illuminating and so hopeful. We invited the group to join a class of undergraduates who were also enrolled in Race and the American Story at Mizzou. When the community group arrived they sat to one side of the room while the undergraduates sat on the other side. We moderated a conversation between the sides and sat back to experience what became a beautiful discussion. They had all read the same readings but their perspectives were very different. During the music exercise, the undergraduates cited Kendrick Lamar and Rage against the Machine, the seasoned community members called out James Brown and Pete Seeger. The younger ones explained their horror at the ways in which even the Founding Fathers had written about Black people; the seasoned ones expressed their memories of how scared they had been in the 1960s when the news stories had framed Malcolm X as a dangerous radical. They contrasted this perception with the Malcolm X speeches they had recently engaged with. And at the end of the conversation, a member of the seasoned group expressed deep regret for not having done more to create a better world for the undergraduates, who were gracious and grateful for the opportunity to experience such a candid and generative conversation. We were all moved, understanding that there is still so much work to do.

The work of combating global racism should not be left to one generation, to one group, to Black folks in Africa or in the Americas. For too long, the focus has been on the oppressed who must persevere, pull themselves up by the bootstrings, forget the history and forgive those who continue to oppress and degrade them. Many people seem to think that all the work of antiracism should be done by those who have suffered the brunt of racism. But the inheritors of racist beliefs and practices must themselves contribute to and colead this work. Justice must include redemption.

Reading the work of scholars like Du Bois and listening to an album like Roach's *We Insist* are essential ways of opening eyes and minds and beginning this redemptive work. It is important to use these texts as a portal to the vision of a liberated community and a just world. From texts like these, we can access a nuanced set of guiding principles that will lead to that better world. For example, the Declaration of Independence presents a lofty vision of US citizenship that we can all agree has not been fully realized. We continue to bring nuance to that, to tease out what should really be meant by that preamble.

And after we have all woken up, it will be time to renew our beliefs and commitment. The commitment to a free and just world, to a world liberated from oppression and united by love, is supported both by the strikingly beautiful musical creations of the African diaspora and by the inspirational American conviction about human freedom. These narrative vehicles, however different in their origins, expressions, and immediate purposes, contain resonating intersections powerful enough to change the world. A world in tune with Black music and inspired by American ideals can, perhaps, finally redeem itself from the tragic failures of its racist past.

Du Bois's Credo, according to his biographer David Levering Lewis, inspired African Americans and was displayed in many African American homes in the 1920s, similar to the impact of King's "I Have a Dream" speech in the 1960s and 1970s. Written in 1904, Du Bois's "Credo" is both simple and complex. It has clear direction and sharp irony. But if one considers the long arc of his career, and the shifts in his ideological leanings, as varied and complicated as the man was, these eight beliefs served as a consistent guiding light. Levering-Lewis explains that the Credo was written to inspire Blacks and calm whites. It is a credo that stands the test of time and can still inspire us all:

1. "I believe in God who made of one blood all races that dwell on earth. I believe that all men, Black and white, are brothers, varying through Time and Opportunity, in form and gift and feature, but differing in no essential particular, and alike in soul and in the possibility of infinite development. Especially do I believe in the Negro Race; in the beauty of its genius, the sweetness of its soul, and its strength in that meekness which shall yet inherit this turbulent earth."

2. "I believe in pride of race and lineage and self; in pride of self so deep as to scorn injustice to other selves; in pride of lineage so great as to despise no man's father; in pride of race so chivalrous as neither to offer bastardy to the weak nor beg wedlock of

the strong, knowing that men may be brothers in Christ, even though they be not brother-in-law."

3. "I believe in Service—humble reverent service, from the blackening of boots to the whitening of souls; for Work is Heaven, Idleness is Hell, and Wage is the 'Well done!' of the Master who summoned all them that labor and are heavy laden, making no distinction between the Black sweating cotton-hands of Georgia and the First Families of Virginia, since all distinction not based on deed is devilish and not divine."

4. "I believe in the Devil and his angels, who wantonly work to narrow the opportunity of struggling human beings, especially if they be Black; who spit in the faces of the fallen, strike them that cannot strike again, believe the worst and work to prove it, hating the image which their Maker stamped on a brother's soul."

5. "I believe in the Prince of Peace. I believe that War is Murder. I believe that armies and navies are at bottom the tinsel and braggadocia of oppression and wrong; and I believe that the wicked conquest of weaker and darker nations by nations whiter and stronger but foreshadows the death of that strength."

6. "I believe in Liberty for all men; the space to stretch their arms and their souls; the right to breathe and the right to vote, the freedom to choose their friends, enjoy the sunshine and ride on the railroads, uncursed by color; thinking, dreaming, working as they will in the kingdom of God and love."

7. "I believe in the training of children, Black even as white; the leading out of little souls into the green pastures and beside the still waters, not for pelf or peace, but for Life lit by some large vision of beauty and goodness and truth; lest we forget, and the sons of the fathers, like Esau, for mere meat barter their birthright in a mighty nation."

8. "Finally, I believe in Patience—patience with the weakness of the Weak and the strength of the Strong, the prejudice of the Ignorant and the ignorance of the Blind; patience with the tardy

triumph of Joy and the mad chastening of Sorrow—patience
with God."

This final item on Du Bois's Credo signifies the importance of hope. This is
why we created the Race and the American Story project. After four hundred years, there is still no magic wand to wipe away all the residual effects
of a violent history. But with patience and careful intention, through different strategies and approaches, there is hope, though tardy, that we can
yet triumph over racism and injustice in our country and our world.

INTRODUCTION

1. Studs Terkel, *Race: How Blacks and Whites Think and Feel about the American Obsession* (New York: The New Press, 1992), 18.
2. David W. McIvor, *Mourning in America: Race and the Politics of Loss* (Ithaca: Cornell University Press, 2016).
3. Gokhan Savas, "Understanding Critical Race Theory as a Framework in Higher Educational Research," *British Journal of Sociology of Education* 35, no. 4 (2014): 506–522.
4. Our course differs, for example, from the kind of periodic collaboration exemplified by Professors Robert George and Cornell West of Princeton University in its extent and depth; and from collaborations such as that between Professors Glisson and Tucker of the William Winter Institute for Racial Reconciliation at the University of Mississippi (https://libraries.olemiss.edu/cedar-archives/finding_aids/MUM00 793.html) in its joining of two academic silos characterized in recent decades by starkly opposed ideologies and very different content.
5. Many educational initiatives, such as "The Welcome Table" at the University of South Carolina (https://sc.edu/uofsc/posts/2017/08/welcome_table.php) or NPR's StoryCorps (https://storycorps.org/partner/npr/), focus on the sharing of personal stories as the basis for building mutual understanding and facilitating dialogue across difference, without the component of extended engagement with historical primary sources.
6. Many of these courses, trainings, and minicourses also focus on narrower contexts of higher education, K–12 education, or other particular workplaces or social contexts, along with a clear direction to immediate practical application. One example of this is Harvard's Bravely Confronting Racism in Higher Education online course: https://www.gse.harvard.edu/ppe/program/bravely-confronting-racism-higher-education?utm_source=olp&utm_medium=web&utm_campaign=bcr.
7. Examples of such organizations include the National Coalition for Dialogue and Deliberation (https://www.ncdd.org/map.html); The Foundation Against Intolerance and Racism (https://www.fairforall.org/); Heterodox Academy (https://heterodoxacademy.org/); and Braver Angels (https://braverangels.org/).

8. Edna Acosta-Belen's *Puerto Ricans in the United States: A Contemporary Portrait*, Paolo Ramos's *Finding Latinx: In Search of the Voices Redefining Latino Identity*.

9. Helen Zia's *Asian American Dreams: The Emergence of an American People*; Khyati Joshi's *Asian Americans in Dixie: Race and Migration in the South*; Timothy Fong's *The Contemporary Asian American Experience*; Lynn Itagaki's *Civil Racism: The 1992 Los Angeles Rebellion and the Crisis of Racial Burnout*.

10. David E. Wilkins and Shelly Hulse Wilkins's *Dismembered: Native Disenrollment and the Battle for Human Rights*; Alex Alvartez's *Native America and the Question of Genocide*; Dylan Robinson's *Hungry Listening*.

CHAPTER 1

1. Eleanor Lee Yates, "More Than Child's Play: North Carolina Professor Explores the History of Dolls and Their Sociological Impact," *Black Issues in Higher Education* 21, no. 3 (2004): 34–.

2. Ntone Edjabe and Akinwumi Adesokan, *FESTAC '77: 2nd World Black and African Festival of Arts and Culture* (Cape Town: Chimurenga, 2019).

3. John Michael Cooper, "People of Color Who Write Classical Music: Recovering 'Lost' Music by Black Composers as Resistance and Revolution," *Black History Bulletin* 82, no. 1 (2019): 20–27.

4. W. E. B. Du Bois, "Of the Sorrow Songs," In *The Souls of Black Folk* (Oxford: Oxford University Press, 2007), 156.

5. Thomas Adams Upchurch, *Race Relations in the United States, 1960–1980* (Westport: Greenwood Press, 2008).

6. Joe R. Feagin, *How Blacks Built America: Labor, Culture, Freedom, and Democracy*, 1st ed. (London: Routledge, 2016).

7. Erika Blacksher and Sean A. Valles, "White Privilege, White Poverty: Reckoning with Class and Race in America," *Hastings Center Report* 51, no. S1 (2021): S51–S57.

8. Victor M. Rios, Nikita Carney, and Jasmine Kelekay, "Ethnographies of Race, Crime, and Justice: Toward a Sociological Double-Consciousness," *Annual Review of Sociology* 43, no. 1 (2017): 493–513.

9. "Children in Single-Parent Families by Race in the United States," Kids Count Data Center, The Annie E. Casey Foundation, December 2020, https://datacenter.kidsco unt.org/data/tables/107-children-in-single-parent-families-by-race#detailed/1/ any/false/871,870,573,869,36,868,867,133,38,35/10,11,9,12,1,185,13/432,431.

10. "Did You Know? Children and Grief Statistics," Children's Grief Awareness Day, Caring Foundation, accessed July 7, 2021, https://www.childrensgriefawarenessday. org/cgad2/pdf/griefstatistics.pdf.

11. "Children in Single-Parent Families by Race in the United States."

12. Debra Umberson et al., "Death of Family Members as an Overlooked Source of Racial Disadvantage in the United States," *Proceedings of the National Academy of Sciences—PNAS* 114, no. 5 (2017): 915–920.

13. Amanda D'Ambrosio, "CDC: Infant Mortality Drifts Lower, but Racial Disparities Persist," MedPage Today (Everyday Health Group, August 1, 2019), https://www. medpagetoday.com/obgyn/pregnancy/81347.

14. Marcus Tullius Cicero, Niall Rudd, and Thomas E. J. Wiedemann, *De legibus.* (Bristol, Avon: Bristol Classical Press, 1987).

15. Frederick Douglass and Nicholas Buccola, *The Essential Douglass: Selected Writings and Speeches* (Indianapolis: Hackett Publishing, 2016), 216–231.

16. Adam Seagrave and Stephanie Shonekan, interview by Trevor Harris, *Thinking Out Loud: "Race and The American Story,"* KBIA: Arts and Culture, November 2, 2017.

17. Lynn England and W. Keith Warner, "W. E. B. Du Bois: Reform, Will, and the Veil," *Social Forces* 91, no. 3 (2013): 955–973.

CHAPTER 2

1. Sabelo J. Ndlovu-Gatsheni and Walter Chambati, *Coloniality of Power in Postcolonial Africa: Myths of Decolonization* (Dakar: African Books Collective, 2013).

2. Ralph Ellison, *Invisible Man* (New York: Vintage Books, 1952), 3.

3. Shina Alima and Iroju Opeyemi Anthony, "No Agreement Today, No Agreement Tomorrow: Fela Anikulapo-Kuti and Human Rights Activism in Nigeria," *Journal of Pan African Studies* 6, no. 4 (2013): 74–94.

4. "(1982) Audre Lorde, 'Learning from the 60s,'" BlackPast, August 12, 2012, https://www.Blackpast.org/african-american-history/1982-audre-lorde-learning-60s/.

5. Studs Terkel, *Race: How Blacks and Whites Think and Feel about the American Obsession* (New York: The New Press, 1992), 11.

6. Jason Lee, "Minstrelsy and the Construction of Race in America," https://library.brown.edu/cds/sheetmusic/afam/minstrelsy.html.

7. "Akata" is a derogatory term that Nigerians use to refer to African Americans.

8. Frederick Douglass, *The Essential Douglass: Selected Writings and Speeches* (Indianapolis: Hackett Publishing Company Inc., 2016), 11.

9. Douglass, *The Essential Douglass,* 5.

10. John Hope Franklin and Alfred Moss Jr., *From Slavery to Freedom: A History of African Americans* (New York: A.A. Knopf, 2000), 141.

11. Frederick Douglass, "The Last Flogging," in *My Bondage and My Freedom* (New York: Miller, Orton & Mulligan, 1855), 233–249.

12. "Infant Mortality," Centers for Disease Control and Prevention (US Department of Health & Human Services, September 10, 2020), https://www.cdc.gov/reproductivehealth/maternalinfanthealth/infantmortality.htm.

13. Richard David and James W. Collins, "Why Does Racial Inequity in Health Persist?," *Journal of Perinatology* 41, no. 2 (2020): 346–350.

14. "Napa, CA Demographics," *AreaVibes,* 2016. https://www.areavibes.com/napa-ca/demographics/.

15. Carmen Lavoie, "Institutional Racism and Individual Agency," *Critical Social Work* 15, no. 1 (2019): 30–40.

16. Lantz Miller Fleming, "Persisting Pan-Institutional Racism," *Philosophy and Social Criticism* 43, no. 7 (2017): 748–774.

17. Ivory A. Toldson, "Transdisciplinary Convergence to Accelerate Strategies to Mitigate Institutional Racism in Criminal Justice, Education, and Health Systems (Editor's Commentary)," *Journal of Negro Education* 89, no. 1 (2020): 1–7.

18. Frederick Douglass, "The Meaning of July Fourth for the Negro," in *Frederick Douglass: Selected Speeches and Writings*, ed. Philip S. Foner (Chicago: Lawrence Hill, 1999), 204.

19. Abraham Lincoln, "House Divided Speech, June 16, 1858," Abraham Lincoln Online, Speeches and Writings, http://www.abrahamlincolnonline.org/lincoln/speeches/house.htm (accessed July 8, 2021).

CHAPTER 3

1. Carol Magee, "It's a Small, White World," in *Africa in the American Imagination* (Jackson: University Press of Mississippi, 2012), 115–138.

2. Luigi Esposito and Laural Finley, "Barack Obama, Racial Progress, and the Future of Race Relations in the United States," *Western Journal of Black Studies* 33, no. 3 (2009): 164–175.

3. Mary E. Weems, "Make America Great Again?," *Qualitative Inquiry* 23, no. 2 (2017): 168–170.

4. "Department of Justice Report Regarding the Criminal Investigation into the Shooting Death of Michael Brown by Ferguson, Missouri Police Officer Darren Wilson," Department of Justice, March 4, 2015, https://www.justice.gov/sites/defa ult/files/opa/press-releases/attachments/2015/03/04/doj_report_on_shooting_ of_michael_brown_1.pdf.

5. Max Roser and Hannah Ritchie, "Homicides," 2013, OurWorldInData.org, https:// ourworldindata.org/homicides.

6. "World Child Hunger Facts," World Hunger News, World Hunger Education Service, accessed June 26, 2021, https://www.worldhunger.org/world-child-hun ger-facts/.

7. "Pepperdine University," *Data USA*, Deloitte and Datawheel, 2019, datausa.io/pro file/university/pepperdine-university.

8. "Quick Facts United States: Race and Hispanic Origin," Census, United States Census Bureau, July 1, 2019, https://www.census.gov/quickfacts/fact/map/US/ PST045219.

9. Michael A. McDonnell, "War and Nationhood: Founding Myths and Historical Realities," in *Remembering the Revolution* (Amherst, MA: University of Massachusetts Press, 2013).

10. Prince Hall, *Prince Hall Petitions for the Abolition of Slavery, 1777*, Petition, From Alpha History, *American History*, https://alphahistory.com/americanrevolution/ prince-hall-abolition-slavery-1777/ (accessed July 8, 2021).

11. https://constitutioncenter.org/the-constitution/historic-document-library/detail/ phillis-wheatley-peters-letter-to-reverend-samuel-occum-february-11-1774.

12. Edward J. Blum and Paul Harvey, *The Color of Christ: The Son of God and the Saga of Race in America* (Chapel Hill: University of North Carolina Press, 2012).

13. Alexander Hamilton, *The Federalist Papers: No. 1, October 27, 1787*, essay, from Yale Law School, *The Avalon Project*, https://avalon.law.yale.edu/18th_century/fed01. asp (accessed July 7, 2021).

14. Abraham Lincoln, "Fragments on Slavery, April 1, 1854," document, from Teaching American History, Abraham Lincoln, https://teachingamericanhistory.org/library/document/fragments-on-slavery/ (accessed July 8, 2021).

15. Brian Dirck, "Changing Perspectives on Lincoln, Race, and Slavery," *Magazine of History* 21, no. 4 (2007): 9–12.

16. Abraham Lincoln, Speech at Springfield, July 17, 1858. https://www.gilderlehrman.org/collection/glc02955.

17. Barry Schwartz, "The Emancipation Proclamation: Lincoln's Many Second Thoughts," *Society (New Brunswick)* 52, no. 6 (2015): 590–603.

18. Abraham Lincoln, Henry Louis Gates, and Donald Yacovone, "A House Divided, Speech at Springfield, Illinois," in *Lincoln on Race and Slavery* (Princeton: Princeton University Press, 2009), 114.

19. Annie Woodley Brown, "Racism and the Christian Church in America: Caught between the Knowledge of Good and Evil," *Social Work in Public Health* 34, no. 1 (2019): 134–144.

20. "Fast Facts: Race/Ethnicity of College Faculty," National Center for Education Statistics, US Department of Education, 2018, https://nces.ed.gov/fastfacts/display.asp?id=61.

21. "The Snail-Like Progress of Blacks in Faculty Ranks of Higher Education," *Journal of Blacks in Higher Education*, no. 62 (2008): 25.

22. "African-American & Black Studies," *Data USA*, Deloitte and Datawheel, 2019, https://datausa.io/profile/cip/african-american-Black-studies.

23. Jaclyn Rodríguez et al., "Engaging Race and Racism for Socially Just Intergroup Relations: The Impact of Intergroup Dialogue on College Campuses in the United States," *Multicultural Education Review* 10, no. 3 (2018): 224–245.

CHAPTER 4

1. Christopher Ojeda and Peter K. Hatemi, "Accounting for the Child in the Transmission of Party Identification," *American Sociological Review* 80, no. 6 (2015): 1150–1174.

2. Kristen Bialik, "5 Facts about Black Americans," Pew Research Center, February 22, 2018, https://www.pewresearch.org/fact-tank/2018/02/22/5-facts-about-Blacks-in-the-u-s/.

3. Frederick Douglass, and Nicholas Buccola, *The Essential Douglass: Selected Writings and Speeches* (Indianapolis: Hackett Publishing Company Inc., 2016), 38.

4. "(1982) Audre Lorde, 'Learning from the 60s,'" BlackPast, August 12, 2012, https://www.Blackpast.org/african-american-history/1982-audre-lorde-learning-60s/.

5. Larry J. Griffin and Kenneth A. Bollen, "What Do These Memories Do? Civil Rights Remembrance and Racial Attitudes," *American Sociological Review* 74, no. 4 (2009): 594–614.

6. Kenneth J. Bindas, "Re-Remembering a Segregated Past: Race in American Memory," *History and Memory* 22, no. 1 (2010): 113–134.

7. D. H. Dilbeck, "An Antislavery Constitution and a Righteous Violence," in *Frederick Douglass: America's Prophet* (Chapel Hill: The University of North Carolina Press, 2018).

8. Baffour Ankomah, "The Gandhi We Did Not Know," *New African (London. 1978)*, no. 565 (2016): 14–15.

9. Cogliano, Francis D. *Thomas Jefferson: Reputation and Legacy* (Edinburgh: Edinburgh University Press, 2006).

10. Ida B. Wells, "Lynching and the Excuse for it," *The Independent* 53, no. 2737, May 16, 1901 (2000): 1133–1136.

11. Kamau Rashid, "Beyond the Fetters of Colonialism: Du Bois, Nkrumah, and a Pan-African Critical Theory," *Equity and Excellence in Education* 52, no. 2–3 (2019): 271–282.

12. Barbara Loomis Jackson, "Race, Education, and the Politics of Fear," *Educational Policy (Los Altos, Calif.)* 22, no. 1 (2008): 130–154.

13. Douglas S. Massey, Jonathan Rothwell, and Thurston Domina, "The Changing Bases of Segregation in the United States," *Annals of the American Academy of Political and Social Science* 626, no. 1 (2009): 74–90; Robert Putnam, "Turning the Corner: What American History Teaches Us about Leadership and Civic Renewal" (presentation, Citizenship and Civic Leadership in America, Tempe, AZ, September 25, 2019).

14. Akira Iriye, Petra Goedde, and William I. Hitchcock, *The Human Rights Revolution: An International History* (Oxford: Oxford University Press, 2012).

15. Frederick Douglass, "The Meaning of July Fourth for the Negro," in *Frederick Douglass: Selected Speeches and Writings*, ed. Philip S. Foner (Chicago: Lawrence Hill, 1999), 196.

16. https://www.nytimes.com/2005/06/14/politics/senate-issues-apology-over-failure-on-lynching-law.html.

17. "91 Percent of Americans Support Criminal Justice Reform, ACLU Polling Finds," ACLU (American Civil Liberties Union, November 16, 2017), https://www.aclu.org/press-releases/91-percent-americans-support-criminal-justice-reform-aclu-polling-finds.

18. Richard Lempert, "A Personal Odyssey toward a Theme: Race and Equality in the United States: 1948–2009," *Law and Society Review* 44, no. 3/4 (2010): 431–462.

19. Andrew Kohut, "From the Archives: 50 Years Ago: Mixed Views about Civil Rights but Support for Selma Demonstrators," Pew Research Center, January 16, 2020, https://www.pewresearch.org/fact-tank/2020/01/16/50-years-ago-mixed-views-about-civil-rights-but-support-for-selma-demonstrators/.

20. "Quick Facts United States: Race and Hispanic Origin." https://www.census.gov/quickfacts/fact/table/US/PST045222.

21. Monica Anderson, "A Rising Share of the U.S. Black Population Is Foreign Born," *Pew Research Center*, April 9, 2015, https://www.pewresearch.org/social-trends/2015/04/09/a-rising-share-of-the-u-s-Black-population-is-foreign-born/.

22. "2010 Census of Population and Housing," Census, US Census Bureau, September, 2012, https://www.census.gov/content/dam/Census/library/publications/2011/dec/c2010br-02.pdf .

23. Abraham Lincoln, Stephen A. Douglas, and Edwin Erle Sparks, "Alton Debate," in *The Lincoln-Douglas Debates of 1858* (Springfield: Published by the Trustees of the Illinois State Historical Library, 1908), 449–510.

24. Garrett Epps, *Democracy Reborn: The Fourteenth Amendment and the Fight for Equal Rights in Post-Civil War America*, 1st ed. (New York: H. Holt, 2006).

25. W. E. B. Du Bois, "Of Our Spiritual Strivings," In *The Souls of Black Folk* (Oxford: Oxford University Press, 2007), 7.

26. Frederick Douglass et al., *The Speeches of Frederick Douglass: A Critical Edition* (New Haven: Yale University Press, 2018), 295.

27. Stephanie has since learned from her self-care-conscious daughter that everyone should use sunscreen no matter their skin tone.

28. Martin Luther King Jr., *I Have a Dream: Writings and Speeches That Changed the World*, ed. James M. Washington (New York: Harper Collins, 1986), 31–32.

29. Martin Luther King Jr., *"I've Been to the Mountaintop", April 3, 1968*, Speech, from American Federation of State, County & Municipal Employees, *MLK*, https://www.afscme.org/about/history/mlk/mountaintop/ (accessed July 8, 2021).

CHAPTER 5

1. Jeffrey L. Pasley, Andrew W. Robertson, and David Waldstreicher, *Beyond the Founders: New Approaches to the Political History of the Early American Republic* (Chapel Hill: University of North Carolina Press, 2004).

2. Joshua A. Claybourn, *Our American Story: The Search for a Shared National Narrative* (Lincoln: Potomac Books, 2019).

3. Frederick Douglass et al., *The Speeches of Frederick Douglass: A Critical Edition* (New Haven: Yale University Press, 2018), 295.

4. David Armitage, *The Declaration of Independence: A Global History* (Cambridge, MA: Harvard University Press, 2008).

5. Simon Henderson, "Flawed Heroes: Washington, Jefferson and Slavery," in *Aspects of American History* (London: Routledge, 2009), 29–38.

6. Paul Kendrick and Stephen Kendrick, *Douglass and Lincoln: How a Revolutionary Black Leader and a Reluctant Liberator Struggled to End Slavery and Save the Union*, 1st US ed. (New York: Walker & Co., 2008).

7. David W. Blight, *Frederick Douglass: Prophet of Freedom* (New York: Simon & Schuster, 2018).

8. Kevin Bruyneel, "The King's Body: The Martin Luther King Jr. Memorial and the Politics of Collective Memory," *History and Memory* 26, no. 1 (2014): 75–108.

9. Teresa Bergman, *Exhibiting Patriotism Creating and Contesting Interpretations of American Historic Sites* (Walnut Creek, CA: Left Coast Press, 2013).

10. Roger Taney, *Dred Scott v. Sandford, March 6, 1857*, Supreme Court case, from Teaching American History, Roger Taney, https://teachingamericanhistory.org/library/document/dred-scott-v-sandford-2/ (accessed July 8, 2021).

11. Richard F. Hamilton, *Miseducating Americans: Distortions of Historical Understanding*, 1st ed. (Somerset: Routledge, 2015).

12. Thomas Jefferson, *A Summary View of the Rights of British America, 1774*, document, from Yale Law School, *The Avalon Project*, https://avalon.law.yale.edu/18th_century/jeffsumm.asp (accessed July 8, 2021).

13. "Some Political Writings of James Otis," Collected by Charles F. Mullett, *University of Missouri Studies* 4 (1929): 257–432, https://press-pubs.uchicago.edu/founders/documents/v1ch13s4.html.

14. Abraham Lincoln, *Fragment on Slavery, July 1, 1854*, document, from National Parks Service, *Lincoln on Slavery*, https://www.nps.gov/liho/learn/historyculture/slavery.htm (accessed July 8, 2021).

15. Prince Hall, *Prince Hall Petitions for the Abolition of Slavery, 1777*, Petition, From Alpha History, *American History*, https://alphahistory.com/americanrevolution/prince-hall-abolition-slavery-1777/ (accessed July 8, 2021).

16. Eric Foner, "Freedom: America's Evolving and Enduring Idea," *Magazine of History* 20, no. 4 (2006): 9–11.

17. Michael Yudanin, *Animal Choice and Human Freedom: On the Genealogy of Self-Determined Action* (Lanham, MD: Lexington Books, 2020).

18. David Ramsay and Lester H. Cohen, *The History of the American Revolution* (Indianapolis: Liberty Classics, 1990).

19. Frank D. Bean, "Growing U.S. Ethnoracial Diversity: A Positive or Negative Societal Dynamic?," *Annals of the American Academy of Political and Social Science* 677, no. 1 (2018): 229–239.

20. Jennifer Pavlick, "Reproducing Patriotism: An Exploration of 'Freedom' in US History Textbooks," *Discourse and Society* 30, no. 5 (2019): 482–502.

21. Peter Gardella, *American Civil Religion: What Americans Hold Sacred* (Cary: Oxford University Press, 2013).

22. W. E. B. Du Bois, *The World and Africa; An Inquiry into the Part Which Africa Has Played in World History* (New York: The Viking Press, 1947), 165.

23. Satnam Virdee and Brendan McGeever, "Racism, Crisis, Brexit," *Ethnic and Racial Studies* 41, no. 10 (2018): 1802–1819.

24. Talib Kweli Greene, "Why #ADOS Is Trash: Receipts Attached," *Medium*, A Medium Corporation, April 10, 2019, https://medium.com/@TalibKweli/why-ados-is-trash-receipts-attached-5a337f46f10.

25. Du Bois, *The World and Africa*, 168.

26. Du Bois, *The World and Africa*, 169.

27. Du Bois, *The World and Africa*, 10–11.

28. Du Bois, *The World and Africa*, 13.

29. W. E. B. Du Bois, *The Souls of Black Folk* (Oxford: Oxford University Press, 2007), 16.

30. Georgia A. Ryder, "Another Look at Some American Cantatas," *The Black Perspective in Music* 3, no.2 (1975): 135–140.

31. Eileen Southern, *The Music of African Americans* (New York: WW Norton, 1997), 295.

32. Samuel Floyd, *The Power of Black Music: Interpreting its History from Africa to the United States* (New York: Oxford University Press, 1995), 110.

33. Eileen Southern, "Conversation with William Grant Still," *Black Perspective in Music* (1975), 167.

34. Ruth Gillum, "The Negro Folksong in the American Culture," *Journal of Negro Education* 12, no. 2 (1943): 180.

35. Olly Wilson, "Black Music as an Art Form," *Black Music Research Journal* (1983): 9.

36. Eileen Southern, *Readings in Black American Music* (New York: WW. Norton, 1983), 94.

37. Arnold Rampersad, *The Art and Imagination of W.E.B. Du Bois* (New York: Schoken Books, 1976), 74.

38. Amiri Baraka, *The Autobiography of LeRoi Jones* (New York: Freudlich Books, 1984), 49.

39. Benjamin Brawley, *The Negro Genius: A New Appraisal of the Achievement of the American Negro in Literature and the Fine Arts* (New York: Biblo and Tannen, 1969), 13.

40. Booker T. Washington, *The Booker T. Washington Papers*, ed. Louis Harlan and Rayond Smock (Chicago: University of Illinois Press, 1974), 373.

41. Booker T. Washington, "The Awakening of the Negro." *The Atlantic Monthly* (1896): 322.

42. W. E. B. Du Bois, *The Souls of Black Folk* (Chicago: A.C. McClurg & Co.), 87.

43. Thomas Durant, Jr., and Joyce S. Louden, "The Black Middle Class in America: Historical and Contemporary Perspectives," *Phylon* 47, no. 4 (1986): 254.

44. Jon Michael Spencer, *The New Negroes and Their Music: The Success of the Harlem Renaissance* (Knoxville: University of Tennessee Press, 1997), 2.

45. Samuel Floyd, *The Power of Black Music: Interpreting its History from Africa to the United States* (New York: Oxford University Press, 1995), 106.

46. Geneva Handy Southall, *Blind Tom the Black Pianist Composer* (Lanham: The Scarecrow Press, 1999), 271.

47. Eileen Southern, *The Music of Black Americans: A History.* (New York: W.W. Norton, 1997), 404–405.

48. Samuel Floyd, *The Power of Black Music: Interpreting its History from Africa to the United States* (New York: Oxford University Press, 1995), 10.

49. Arna Bontemps, *Harlem Renaissance Remembered* (New York: Dodd Mead and Company, 1972), 5.

50. Karen McCarthy Brown, *Mama Lola: A Vodou Priestess in Brooklyn* (Berkley: University of California Press, 1993).

51. Leslie H. Fischel, "The Genteel Tradition: Black, Beautiful and Breaking Down," *Reviews in American History* 19, no. 3 (1991): 381.

52. E. Franklin Frazier, *Black Bourgeoisie* (Glencoe: The Free Press, 1957), 237–238.

53. Portia Maultsby and Mellonee Burnim, *African American Music: An Introduction* (New York: Routledge, 2014), 577.

54. Benjamin Brawley. *The Negro Genius: A New Appraisal of the Achievement of the American Negro in Literature and the Fine Arts* (New York: Biblo and Tannen, 1969), 13–14.

55. Ian Rocksborough-Smith, "Black-History Activism and the Afro-American Heritage Association," in *Black Public History in Chicago: Civil Rights Activism from World War II into the Cold War* (Urbana: University of Illinois Press, 2018), 83.

56. Rocksborough-Smith, "Black-History Activism and the Afro-American Heritage Association," 83.
57. Steve Futterman, "Max Roach's We Insist, " *JAZZed* 10, no. 4 (2015): 38.
58. Alisa White, "'We Insist! Freedom Now': Max Roach's Transatlantic Civil Rights Imperative," *Jazz Education Journal* 40, no. 2–3 (2007): 47–52.
59. Fred Moten, *In the Break: The Aesthetics of the Black Radical Tradition* (Minneapolis: University of Minnesota Press, 2003), 22.
60. Moten, *In the Break*, 22.
61. Nicholas Cook and Richard Pettengill, *Taking It to the Bridge: Music as Performance* (Ann Arbor: University of Michigan Press, 2013), 141.
62. Du Bois, *Souls of Black Folk*, 78.

BIBLIOGRAPHY

Acosta-Belen, Edna. *Puerto Ricans in the United States: A Contemporary Portrait*. Boulder, CO: Lynne Rienner Publishers, 2006.

"African-American & Black Studies." *Data USA*, Deloitte and Datawheel, 2019, https://datausa.io/profile/cip/african-american-Black-studies.

Alimi, Shina, and Iroju Opeyemi Anthony. "No Agreement Today, No Agreement Tomorrow: Fela Anikulapo-Kuti and Human Rights Activism in Nigeria." *Journal of Pan African Studies* 6, no. 4 (2013): 74–94.

Anderson, Monica. "A Rising Share of the U.S. Black Population Is Foreign Born." Pew Research Center, April 9, 2015. https://www.pewresearch.org/social-trends/2015/04/09/a-rising-share-of-the-u-s-Black-population-is-foreign-born/.

Ankomah, Baffour. "The Gandhi We Did Not Know." *New African (London. 1978)*, no. 565 (2016): 14–15.

Armitage, David. *The Declaration of Independence: A Global History*. Cambridge, MA: Harvard University Press, 2008.

Bean, Frank D. "Growing U.S. Ethnoracial Diversity: A Positive or Negative Societal Dynamic?" *Annals of the American Academy of Political and Social Science* 677, no. 1 (2018): 229–239.

Bergman, Teresa. *Exhibiting Patriotism Creating and Contesting Interpretations of American Historic Sites*. Walnut Creek, CA: Left Coast Press, 2013.

Bialik, Kristen. "5 Facts about Black Americans." Pew Research Center, February 22, 2018. https://www.pewresearch.org/fact-tank/2018/02/22/5-facts-about-Blacks-in-the-u-s/.

Bindas, Kenneth J. "Re-Remembering a Segregated Past: Race in American Memory." *History and Memory* 22, no. 1 (2010): 113–134.

Blacksher, Erika, and Sean A. Valles. "White Privilege, White Poverty: Reckoning with Class and Race in America." *Hastings Center Report* 51, no. S1 (2021): S51–S57.

Blight, David W. *Frederick Douglass: Prophet of Freedom*. First Simon & Schuster hardcover ed. New York: Simon & Schuster, 2018.

Blum, Edward J., and Paul Harvey. *The Color of Christ: The Son of God and the Saga of Race in America*. Chapel Hill: University of North Carolina Press, 2012.

Brown, Annie Woodley. "Racism and the Christian Church in America: Caught between the Knowledge of Good and Evil." *Social Work in Public Health* 34, no. 1
(2019): 134–144.

Bruyneel, Kevin. "The King's Body: The Martin Luther King Jr. Memorial and the
Politics of Collective Memory." *History and Memory* 26, no. 1 (2014): 75–108.

"Children in Single-Parent Families by Race in the United States." Kids Count Data
Center. The Annie E. Casey Foundation, December 2020. https://datacenter.kidsco
unt.org/data/tables/107-children-in-single-parent-families-by-race#detailed/1/any/
false/871,870,573,869,36,868,867,133,38,35/10,11,9,12,1,185,13/432,431.

Cicero, Marcus Tullius, Niall Rudd, and Thomas E. J. Wiedemann. *De legibus.* I. I.
Bristol, Avon: Bristol Classical Press, 1987.

Claybourn, Joshua A. *Our American Story: The Search for a Shared National Narrative.*
Lincoln: Potomac Books, 2019.

Cook, Nicholas, and Richard Pettengill. *Taking It to the Bridge: Music as Performance.*
Ann Arbor: University of Michigan Press, 2013.

Cooper, John Michael. "People of Color Who Write Classical Music: Recovering 'Lost'
Music by Black Composers as Resistance and Revolution." *Black History Bulletin* 82,
no. 1 (2019): 20–27.

David, Richard, and James W. Collins. "Why Does Racial Inequity in Health Persist?,"
Journal of Perinatology 41, no. 2 (2020): 346–350.

Department of Justice. "Department of Justice Report Regarding the Criminal
Investigation into the Shooting Death of Michael Brown by Ferguson, Missouri
Police Officer Darren Wilson." March 4, 2015. https://www.justice.gov/sites/default/
files/opa/press-releases/attachments/2015/03/04/doj_report_on_shooting_of_mich
ael_brown_1.pdf.

"Did You Know? Children and Grief Statistics." Children's Grief Awareness Day. Caring
Foundation, accessed July 7, 2021. https://www.childrensgriefawarenessday.org/
cgad2/pdf/griefstatistics.pdf.

Dilbeck, D. H. *Frederick Douglass: America's Prophet.* Chapel Hill: University of North
Carolina Press, 2018.

Dirck, Brian. "Changing Perspectives on Lincoln, Race, and Slavery." *Magazine of
History* 21, no. 4 (2007): 9–12.

Douglass, Frederick. *My Bondage and My Freedom.* New York: Miller, Orton &
Mulligan, 1855.

Douglass, Frederick. "The Meaning of July Fourth for the Negro." In *Frederick
Douglass: Selected Speeches and Writings*, edited by Philip S. Foner, 188–206.
Chicago: Lawrence Hill, 1999.

Douglass, Frederick, and Nicholas Buccola. *The Essential Douglass: Selected Writings
and Speeches.* Indianapolis: Hackett Publishing, 2016.

Douglass, Frederick, John R. McKivigan, Julie Husband, and Heather L. Kaufman.
The Speeches of Frederick Douglass: A Critical Edition. New Haven: Yale University
Press, 2018.

"Do You Think New Civil Rights Laws Are Needed to Reduce Discrimination against
Lesbian, Gay, Bisexual or Transgender People, or Not?" Gallup News. Gallup, Inc.,
2019. https://news.gallup.com/poll/1651/gay-lesbian-rights.aspx.

Du Bois, W. E. B. *The Souls of Black Folk*, –. Oxford: Oxford University Press, 2007.

Du Bois, W. E. B. *The World and Africa: An Inquiry into the Part Which Africa Has Played in World History*. New York: Viking Press, 1947.

Edjabe, Ntone, and Akinwumi Adesokan. *FESTAC '77: 2nd World Black and African Festival of Arts and Culture*. Cape Town: Chimurenga, 2019.

Ellison, Ralph. *Invisible Man*. New York: Vintage Books, 1952.

England, Lynn, and W. Keith Warner. "W. E. B. Du Bois: Reform, Will, and the Veil." *Social Forces* 91, no. 3 (2013): 955–973.

Epps, Garrett. *Democracy Reborn: The Fourteenth Amendment and the Fight for Equal Rights in Post–Civil War America*. 1st ed. New York: H. Holt, 2006.

Esposito, Luigi, and Laural Finley. "Barack Obama, Racial Progress, and the Future of Race Relations in the United States." *Western Journal of Black Studies* 33, no. 3 (2009): 164–175.

"Fast Facts: Race/Ethnicity of College Faculty." National Center for Education Statistics. US Department of Education, 2018. https://nces.ed.gov/fastfacts/display.asp?id=61.

Feagin, Joe R. *How Blacks Built America: Labor, Culture, Freedom, and Democracy*. 1st ed. London: Routledge, 2016.

Fleming, Miller Lantz. "Persisting Pan-Institutional Racism." *Philosophy and Social Criticism* 43, no. 7 (2017): 748–774.

Foner, Eric. "Freedom: America's Evolving and Enduring Idea." *Magazine of History* 20, no. 4 (2006): 9–11.

Fong, Timothy. *The Contemporary Asian American Experience*. London: Pearson, 2020.

Franklin, John Hope, and Alfred Moss Jr. *From Slavery to Freedom: A History of African Americans*. New York: A. A. Knopf, 2000.

Futterman, Steve. "Max Roach's *We Insist*." *JAZZed* 10, no. 4 (2015): 38.

Gardella, Peter. *American Civil Religion: What Americans Hold Sacred*. Cary: Oxford University Press, 2013.

Griffin, Larry J., and Kenneth A. Bollen. "What Do These Memories Do? Civil Rights Remembrance and Racial Attitudes." *American Sociological Review* 74, no. 4 (2009): 594–614.

Hall, Prince. *Prince Hall Petitions for the Abolition of Slavery, 1777*. Petition. Alpha History, *American History*. https://alphahistory.com/americanrevolution/prince-hall-abolition-slavery-1777/ (accessed July 8, 2021).

Hamilton, Alexander. *The Federalist Papers: No. 1, October 27, 1787*, edited by Clinton Rossiter. New York: Signet, 2003.

Hamilton, Richard F. *Miseducating Americans: Distortions of Historical Understanding*. 1st ed. Somerset: Routledge, 2015.

Henderson, Simon. "Flawed Heroes: Washington, Jefferson and Slavery." In *Aspects of American History*, edited by Simon Henderson, 45–53. London: Routledge, 2009.

"Infant Mortality." Centers for Disease Control and Prevention. US Department of Health & Human Services, September 10, 2020. https://www.cdc.gov/reproductivehealth/maternalinfanthealth/infantmortality.htm.

Itagaki, Lynn. *Civil Racism: The 1992 Los Angeles Rebellion and the Crisis of Racial Burnout*. Minneapolis: University of Minnesota Press, 2016.

Iriye, Akira, Petra Goedde, and William I. Hitchcock. *The Human Rights Revolution: An International History* Oxford: Oxford University Press, 2012.

Jackson, Barbara Loomis. "Race, Education, and the Politics of Fear." *Educational Policy (Los Altos, Calif.)* 22, no. 1 (2008): 130–154.

Jefferson, Thomas. *A Summary View of the Rights of British America, 1774.* Document. Yale Law School, *The Avalon Project.* https://avalon.law.yale.edu/18th_century/jeffsumm.asp (accessed July 8, 2021).

Joshi, Khyati. *Asian Americans in Dixie: Race and Migration in the South.* Champaign: University of Illinois Press, 2013.

Kendrick, Paul, and Stephen Kendrick. *Douglass and Lincoln: How a Revolutionary Black Leader and a Reluctant Liberator Struggled to End Slavery and Save the Union.* 1st US ed. New York: Walker & Co., 2008.

King, Martin Luther, Jr. *"I've Been to the Mountaintop," April 3, 1968.* Speech. American Federation of State, County & Municipal Employees, *MLK.* https://www.afscme.org/about/history/mlk/mountaintop/ (accessed July 8, 2021).

King, Martin Luther, Jr. *I Have a Dream: Writings and Speeches That Changed the World.* Edited by James M. Washington, 31–32. New York: Harper Collins, 1986.

Kohut, Andrew. "From the Archives: 50 Years Ago: Mixed Views about Civil Rights But Support for Selma Demonstrators." Pew Research Center, January 16, 2020. https://www.pewresearch.org/fact-tank/2020/01/16/50-years-ago-mixed-views-about-civil-rights-but-support-for-selma-demonstrators/.

Kweli Greene, Talib. "Why #ADOS Is Trash. Receipts Attached." *Medium.* A Medium Corporation, April 10, 2019. https://medium.com/@TalibKweli/why-ados-is-trash-receipts-attached-5a337f46f10.

Lavoie, Carmen. "Institutional Racism and Individual Agency." *Critical Social Work* 15, no. 1 (2019): 30–40.

Lempert, Richard. "A Personal Odyssey toward a Theme: Race and Equality in the United States: 1948–2009." *Law and Society Review* 44, no. 3/4 (2010): 431–462.

Lincoln, Abraham. *Fragment on Slavery, July 1, 1854.* Document. National Parks Service, *Lincoln on Slavery.* https://www.nps.gov/liho/learn/historyculture/slavery.htm (accessed July 8, 2021).

Lincoln, Abraham. *Fragments on Slavery, April 1, 1854.* Document. Teaching American History, *Abraham Lincoln.* https://teachingamericanhistory.org/library/document/fragments-on-slavery/ (accessed July 8, 2021).

Lincoln, Abraham. *House Divided Speech, June 16, 1858.* Speech. Abraham Lincoln Online, *Speeches and Writings.* http://www.abrahamlincolnonline.org/lincoln/speeches/house.htm (accessed July 8, 2021).

Lincoln, Abraham, Stephen A. Douglas. "Alton Debate." In *The Lincoln-Douglas Debates of 1858,* edited by Edwin Erle Sparks, 449–510. Springfield: Published by the Trustees of the Illinois State Historical Library, 1908.

Lincoln, Abraham. "A House Divided, Speech at Springfield, Illinois." In *Lincoln on Race and Slavery,* edited by Henry Louis Gates and Donald Yacovone, 114–116. Princeton: Princeton University Press, 2009.

Magee, Carol. *Africa in the American Imagination.* Jackson: University Press of Mississippi, 2012.

Massey, Douglas S., Jonathan Rothwell, and Thurston Domina. "The Changing Bases of Segregation in the United States." *Annals of the American Academy of Political and Social Science* 626, no. 1 (2009): 74–90.

Michael A. McDonnell, Clare Corbould, Frances M. Clarke, W. Fitzhugh Brundage, eds. *Remembering the Revolution.* Amherst: University of Massachusetts Press, 2013.

McIvor, David W. *Mourning in America: Race and the Politics of Loss.* Ithaca, NY: Cornell University Press, 2016.

Moten, Fred. *In the Break: The Aesthetics of the Black Radical Tradition.* Minneapolis: University of Minnesota Press, 2003.

"Napa, CA Demographics." *AreaVibes.* AreaVibes Inc., 2016. https://www.areavibes. com/napa-ca/demographics/.

Ndlovu-Gatsheni, Sabelo J., and Walter Chambati. *Coloniality of Power in Postcolonial Africa: Myths of Decolonization.* Dakar: African Books Collective, 2013.

Nelson, Michael, Michael Berkman, and Eric Plutzer. "Poll Report: Americans Divided on Wedding Services Conflicts." McCourtney Institute for Democracy. Pennsylvania State University, November 30, 2017. https://democracy.psu.edu/poll-report-archive/ poll-report-americans-divided-on-wedding-services-conflicts/.

"(1982) Audre Lorde, 'Learning from the 60s.'" *BlackPast.* BlackPast.org, August 12, 2012. https://www.Blackpast.org/african-american-history/1982-audre-lorde-learn ing-60s/.

"91 Percent of Americans Support Criminal Justice Reform, ACLU Polling Finds." ACLU. American Civil Liberties Union, November 16, 2017. https://www.aclu.org/ press-releases/91-percent-americans-support-criminal-justice-reform-aclu-poll ing-finds.

Ojeda, Christopher, and Peter K. Hatemi. "Accounting for the Child in the Transmission of Party Identification." *American Sociological Review* 80, no. 6 (2015): 1150–1174.

Pasley, Jeffrey L., Andrew W. Robertson, and David Waldstreicher. *Beyond the Founders: New Approaches to the Political History of the Early American Republic.* Chapel Hill: University of North Carolina Press, 2004.

Pavlick, Jennifer. "Reproducing Patriotism: An Exploration of 'Freedom' in US History Textbooks." *Discourse and Society* 30, no. 5 (2019): 482–502.

"Pepperdine University." *Data USA,* Deloitte and Datawheel, 2019, datausa.io/profile/ university/pepperdine-university.

Putnam, Robert. "Turning the Corner: What American History Teaches Us about Leadership and Civic Renewal." Presented at Citizenship and Civic Leadership in America, Tempe, AZ, September 25, 2019.

Ramos, Paolo. *Finding Latinx: In Search of the Voices Redefining Latino Identity.* NY: Vintage, 2020.

Ramsay, David, and Lester H. Cohen. *The History of the American Revolution.* Indianapolis: Liberty Classics, 1990.

Rashid, Kamau. "Beyond the Fetters of Colonialism: Du Bois, Nkrumah, and a Pan-African Critical Theory." *Equity and Excellence in Education* 52, no. 2–3 (2019): 271–282.

Rios, Victor M., Nikita Carney, and Jasmine Kelekay. "Ethnographies of Race, Crime, and Justice: Toward a Sociological Double-Consciousness." *Annual Review of Sociology* 43, no. 1 (2017): 493–513.

Rocksborough-Smith, Ian *Black Public History in Chicago: Civil Rights Activism from World War II into the Cold War*, 75–100. Urbana: University of Illinois Press, 2018.

Rodríguez, Jaclyn, Biren (Ratnesh) A. Nagda, Nicholas Sorensen, and Patricia Gurin. "Engaging Race and Racism for Socially Just Intergroup Relations: The Impact of Intergroup Dialogue on College Campuses in the United States." *Multicultural Education Review* 10, no. 3 (2018): 224–245.

Roser, Max, and Hannah Ritchie. "Homicides." *OurWorldInData.org*. 2013. https://our worldindata.org/homicides.

Savas, Gokhan. "Understanding Critical Race Theory as a Framework in Higher Educational Research." *British Journal of Sociology of Education* 35, no. 4 (2014): 506–522.

Schwartz, Barry. "The Emancipation Proclamation: Lincoln's Many Second Thoughts." *Society (New Brunswick)* 52, no. 6 (2015): 590–603.

Seagrave, Adam, and Stephanie Shonekan. *Thinking Out Loud: "Race and the American Story."* By Trevor Harris. KBIA: Arts and Culture, November 2, 2017.

Selby, Gary S. "Mocking the Sacred: Frederick Douglass's 'Slaveholder's Sermon' and the Antebellum Debate over Religion and Slavery." *Quarterly Journal of Speech* 88, no. 3 (2002): 326–341.

"Senate Passes a Resolution Apologizing for Failure to Pass Anti-Lynching Legislation." *Jet* 108, no. 1 (2005): 8.

Cogliano, Francis D. *Thomas Jefferson: Reputation and Legacy*. Edinburgh: Edinburgh University Press, 2013.

"Some Political Writings of James Otis." Collected by Charles F. Mullett. *University of Missouri Studies* 4 (1929): 257–432. https://press-pubs.uchicago.edu/founders/documents/v1ch13s4.html.

Taney, Roger. *Dred Scott v. Sandford, March 6, 1857*. Supreme Court Case. Teaching American History, *Roger Taney*. https://teachingamericanhistory.org/library/document/dred-scott-v-sandford-2/ (accessed July 8, 2021).

Terkel, Studs. *Race: How Blacks and Whites Think and Feel about the American Obsession*. New York: The New Press, 1992.

"The Snail-Like Progress of Blacks in Faculty Ranks of Higher Education." *Journal of Blacks in Higher Education*, no. 62 (Winter 2008): 24–25.

Toldson, Ivory A. "Transdisciplinary Convergence to Accelerate Strategies to Mitigate Institutional Racism in Criminal Justice, Education, and Health Systems (Editor's Commentary)." *Journal of Negro Education* 89, no. 1 (2020): 1–7.

"2010 Census of Population and Housing." Census. United States Census Bureau, September 2012. https://www.census.gov/library/publications/2012/dec/cph-2.html.

Umberson, Debra, Julie Skalamera Olson, Robert Crosnoe, Hui Liu, Tetyana Pudrovska, and Rachel Donnelly. "Death of Family Members as an Overlooked Source of Racial Disadvantage in the United States." *Proceedings of the National Academy of Sciences* 114, no. 5 (2017): 915–920.

Upchurch, Thomas Adams. *Race Relations in the United States, 1960–1980*. Westport, CT: Greenwood Press, 2008.

Virdee, Satnam, and Brendan McGeever. "Racism, Crisis, Brexit." *Ethnic and Racial Studies* 41, no. 10 (2018): 1802–1819.

Weems, Mary E. "Make America Great Again?" *Qualitative Inquiry* 23, no. 2 (2017): 168–170.

Wells, Ida B. "Lynching and the Excuse for It." *The Independent* 53, no. 2737, May 16, 1901, pp. 1133–1136 (2000).

White, Alisa. "'We Insist! Freedom Now': Max Roach's Transatlantic Civil Rights Imperative." *Jazz Education Journal* 40, no. 2–3 (2007): 47–52.

Wilkins, David E., and Shelly Hulse Wilkins. *Dismembered: Native Disenrollment and the Battle for Human Rights*. Seattle: University of Washington Press, 2017.

Wilson, Joshua C. *The Street Politics of Abortion: Speech, Violence, and America's Culture Wars*. Stanford: Stanford Law Books, an imprint of Stanford University Press, 2013.

"World Child Hunger Facts." World Hunger News. World Hunger Education Service. https://www.worldhunger.org/world-child-hunger-facts/ (accessed June 26, 2021).

Yates, Eleanor Lee. "More Than Child's Play: North Carolina Professor Explores the History of Dolls and Their Sociological Impact." *Black Issues in Higher Education* 21, no. 3 (2004): 34–35.

Yu, Nilan. *Consciousness-Raising: Critical Pedagogy and Practice for Social Change*. 1st ed. Milton: Routledge, 2018.

Yudanin, Michael. *Animal Choice and Human Freedom: On the Genealogy of Self-Determined Action*. Lanham, MD: Lexington Books, 2020.

Zia, Helen. *Asian American Dreams: The Emergence of an American People*. New York: FSG, 2001.

INDEX

For the benefit of digital users, indexed terms that span two pages (e.g., 52–53) may, on occasion, appear on only one of those pages.